W9-BFQ-145

The Practical Meditator

The Practical Meditator

Harry C. Meserve, D. D.

 **HUMAN SCIENCES PRESS**

72 Fifth Avenue   3 Henrietta Street
NEW YORK, NY 10011 ● LONDON, WC2E 8LU

Printed in the United States of America
123456789 987654321

Library of Congress Cataloging in Publication Data

Meserve, Harry C
   The practical meditator.

   Bibliography: p. 131
   Includes index.
   1.   Meditation.   I.   Title.
BL627.M47   291.4′ 3   LC 80–15631
ISBN 0–87705–506–8

Contents

Acknowledgments

My thanks to my wife Kay for invaluable practical help in preparing this manuscript and also for her encouragement in my practice of meditation.

Grateful acknowledgment is made to the following sources for permission to use quotations from copyright material in this volume:

Curtis Brown Ltd.: *The Exploits of the Incomparable Mulla Nasrudin*, by Idries Shah, copyright 1972 by Mulla Nasrudin Enterprises.

Arthur Foote: *Taking Down the Defenses*, Essex Publishing Co., Essex, Vt., 1972.

Harcourt Brace Jovanovich: *The Psychology of Consciousness*, by Robert Ornstein, 1972; "Little Gidding," in *Four Quartets*, copyright 1943 by T. S. Eliot, renewed 1971 by Esme Valerie Eliot.

Harper & Row: *The Perennial Philosophy*, by Aldous Huxley, 1945; *Meister Eckhart: A Modern Translation*, by R. B. Blakney; *The Choice Is Always Ours*, edited by Dorothy Berkley Phillips, 1948; *The Way of Life According to Lao-Tzu*, translated by Witter Bynner, copyright 1944 by Witter Bynner.

Julian Press: *The Cloud of Unknowing*, translated and with introductory commentary by Ira Progoff, copyright 1957 by Ira Progoff.

Alfred A. Knopf, Inc.: *Collected Poems of Wallace Stevens*, copyright 1942 by Wallace Stevens.

J. B. Lippincott Company: *Mysticism and Philosophy*, by W. T. Stace, copyright 1960 by W. T. Stace.

Little, Brown and Company: *How to Meditate: A Guide to Self-Discovery*, by Lawrence LeShan, 1957.

Luzac and Company, Ltd: *Readings from the Mystics of Islam*, by Margaret Smith, 1950.

The Macmillan Publishing Company: "Sailing to Byzantium," in *The Collected Poems of William Butler Yeats*, copyright 1928 by Macmillan, renewed 1956 by Georgia Yeats.

New Directions: *Siddhartha*, by Hermann Hesse, translated by Hilda Rosner, copyright 1951 by New Directions Publishing Corporation.

Oxford University Press: *On Science, Necessity, and the Love of God*, by Simone Weil, copyright 1968.

Ira Progoff: *The Well and the Cathedral*, by Ira Progoff, published by Dialogue House Library, 1971.

Random House: *Memories, Dreams, Reflections*, by C. G. Jung, translated by Richard and Clara Winston, edited by Aniela Jaffe, copyright 1962, 1963 by Random House, Inc., reprinted by permission of Pantheon Books, a division of Random House, Inc.

Simon and Schuster: *The Open Mind*, by J. Robert Oppenheimer, 1955.

The Viking Press, Inc.: *On the Psychology of Meditation*, by Claudio Naranjo and Robert E. Ornstein, 1971.

Careful effort has been made to trace the ownership of all copyright material quoted. If any copyrights have been inadvertently infringed upon, the author offers his apologies and will be pleased to make proper acknowledgment in any future printing.

Introduction

Some years ago, on a visit to Japan and other far Eastern countries, I had occasion to talk with a number of religious leaders in various sects and to look thoughtfully at some of the personal meditative paths taught and practiced by them. In Kyoto and Tokyo I met a number of wise and experienced Zen masters. These men were unfailingly polite and friendly, but they were not helpful in responding to my mission, which I now realize was both ignorant and naïve. At that time I cherished the hope that I could persuade one or more of these masters to prepare a brief, written introduction to meditation, and to Zen meditation in particular, for readers of the Western world who were beginning to show, in increasing numbers, a lively interest in Eastern systems of meditation. In summary, the reply of all these men was, "Thanks, but no thanks." One of them smilingly said, "It is not necessary to write anything about Zen. If anybody wants to learn, he can come here and spend some years with me. I shall be glad to tell him anything I know." I looked at his American student who had then been with the master for twelve years and realized that one could indeed do what he was doing if one really wanted to know. But how many Westerners are there who can or would give up that many years to learning anything? There have been, of course, a few, and we are indebted today to them for their writing and teaching. One of them is the very student who sat with me that day, who introduced me to his master. He has now become a teacher of Zen, a master, in this country.

But most Westerners want their Zen as they want everything else—as swiftly and easily as possible. They want "instant Zen," just as they drink instant coffee and tea. On the same visit to Kyoto I met a professor of psychology who, for a substantial fee, was offering a crash course which he actually called "Instant Zen." His contention was that the essence of Zen could be taught in a single, intensive weekend experience with a group of seekers and a teacher. I gather it was something like the various kinds of encounter group experiences so popular in this country in recent years. Such experiences, whatever their orientation and goal, can have an intensity that is startling and revealing. But they cannot substitute for the slow, steady growth of the intellectual and volitional muscles that is central in meditative experience. I did not take the course in "Instant Zen." Maybe it is still available. Failing that, there are many other courses in instant enlightenment of one sort or another readily available in this country and abroad. If that is what the reader is seeking, what follows here cannot help him very much. It may even discourage him. I advise him to look elsewhere.

But I did, at length, yield to my own request and try to prepare a brief introduction of meditation as a science and an art of life that might be useful to the thoughtful seeker. I have called it *The Practical Meditator*, after two illustrious predecessors: Nathaniel Bowditch's *Practical Navigator* and the more recent volume, *The Practical Cogitator or The Thinker's Anthology*, selected and edited by Charles P. Curtis, Jr., and Ferris Greenslet. Navigation, thinking, meditation all seem to me to have something in common. They are concerned with the means of finding your way across a vast, deep, and largely unexplored area, where what is known is very small compared to the size of what is not known. Such guides as are offered are not very detailed. Rather, they are ways of finding out where you are, what your goals are, and how you may hope to advance toward them. They do not offer detailed plans of the journey or final answers of any kind—just enough to help you find your bearings, set your course, and get on with the journey. The rest is up to the intelligence, the persistence, and the vision of the traveler, equipped with a few essential bits of knowledge and some basic skills.

I am a member of no esoteric cult or sect, religious or psychological. I am nobody's guru or spiritual master. I cannot name any spiritual master of my own, although I think I have learned something of importance from many different people of numerous religions and schools of thought. I make no claim to having arrived at any final meditative goals. If I have experienced something like satori or enlightenment or fulfillment, it is only in brief and fleeting glimpses—enough to keep me on the journey, but not enough to make me think I have arrived anywhere.

About the only truth I can offer as an inducement to embarking on the meditative voyage is the assurance that anybody who undertakes it seriously and patiently will find there is much more within and beyond the range of his own small mind and consciousness than he has ever dreamed possible.

1

Meditation–Why?

Historians have noted that cultures in the process of radical transition and decline tend to produce a variety of new or rediscovered religious movements. The reason is simple enough. As our sense of material security and continued growth in affluence declines, we begin looking for other kinds of security. As the traditional institutions and their objects of reverence and loyalty lose their hold over our minds, we seek other and more personal sources of strength. The first centuries of the Christian era, for example, saw the beginnings of Christianity as a series of small, deeply committed groups of people preserving the memory of Jesus' life, death, and resurrection and looking forward to his imminent return. The first Christians were drop-outs from the surrounding Roman and Jewish societies. They put their hopes elsewhere than in the continuation of the external world, and they suffered persecution for their faith and loyalty to their dream. The Christian groups were not the only representatives of a new religion of personal salvation. There were many others, generally known as "mystery religions." These cults were centered around various myths and gods from the old cultures of the Mediterranean world: Dionysius, Apollo, Orpheus, Isis, and Osiris. Mithras, the Persian sun-god, inspired a cult which many have said was Christianity's chief competitor.

Other forms of personal enlightenment and salvation, especially among intellectuals, were the ancient philosophies of Stoicism, Epicureanism, and Neo-Platonism. The so-called Gnostic groups, of which there were many, claimed to possess certain secret truths that, if known and understood, could preserve the individual from the confusion and destruction all around him and assure him salvation and peace.

Some of these groups had actually found important and permanent truths about the soul and the human condition. Their teachers were wise and sincere men who yearned for a better life for themselves and others. Inevitably, there were also crackpots and charlatans, people who exploited the prevailing religious hunger for their own purposes of power, wealth, or fame.

A similar historic period might be the 15th and 16th centuries, which we usually describe as the Renaissance and the Reformation. A tremendous explosion in human knowledge that involved the age of discovery, the invention of printing, the laying of the foundations of modern science and humanistic expression in the arts also led to the break-up of a religious establishment which had prevailed over Western Europe for 1,000 years. New cults and religious interpretations appeared on every side. It was important, but very difficult, for thoughtful people to judge carefully between truth and falsehood, between the authentic teacher and the charlatan or deceiver. Such judgments were the more difficult because the spirit of religious freedom was just being born into a world where persecution and suppression had ruled for thousands of years.

It seems that we are living in these last years of the 20th century in a somewhat similar period. There are many differences, of course. Major shifts of thought and feeling in a country like ours involve the whole world, and the changes that are taking place are global rather than local. Total destruction is a human potentiality, not a supernatural threat. Asiatic lands to which we were sending Christian missionaries a hundred years ago are now sending missionaries to us. They come from India, China, Japan, Korea, and from other lands. These missionaries appear to have about the same mixture of motives and messages as those Christian ones we sent to Asia. If ever it was necessary to think critically and rationally about what is going on in the religious world and the groups that offer to lead us to personal growth and fulfillment, that time is now.

To begin then, we see ourselves as living in a century which has been enormously creative in the realm of the physical sciences: physics, astronomy, chemistry, biology, mathematics, and the whole realm of communications. Men have stood on the moon and looked at the earth, an undreamt-of experience in earlier ages. Our scientific instruments have explored Mars. Men can send their voices and the images of their actions in pictures that can be broadcast around the world. They have explored the far reaches of space and the unimaginably small spaces of the atom. It all depends on your point of view as to what is small or large. At the same time, we have already witnessed in this century outbreaks of cruelty and destruction of a scope unparalleled in history: the death camps of the Nazis; saturation bombing of cities as an accepted part of warfare; the destruction of two Japanese cities by atom bombs dropped, God forgive us, by Americans; the recurrence of torture and terror and political assassination in many parts of the world as ways of life; and the failure of the so-called civilized countries like our own to protest or renounce them. There have been profound disappointments for people of good will in the 20th century: the failure of democracy to win the minds of men; the inability of an international organization to control nationalistic greed and pride; the incapacity, so far, of any form of society— communist, capitalist, or anything in between—to find solutions to such age-old enemies as hunger, poverty, racial hatred, and war; the frustration we feel as we consider the size and complexity of such recently recognized threats to survival as overpopulation and the deteriorating environment. Finally, there is the uneasiness and anxiety in late 20th-century life as people, old and young, abandon traditional moralities, the established standards of law and loyalty to family, community, church, and school, and go forth in search of new truths and new guides for personal development. It is not hard to understand what prompts the hunger and the search; but it is terrifying to consider, since the possibilities are so mixed between what is true and false, good and evil, beautiful and ugly, the dangers of making wrong choices. Yet this spiritual unrest with all its dangers is perhaps the most hopeful fact of the late 20th century. We are in better condition than we would be if our culture were simply grinding along its traditional way on paths that have led to destruction in the past and can only do so more certainly in the future. It seems that our political leaders, or at least most of them, are still bemused and imprisoned by those paths of power. But we must recall that political power structures, along with the economic and military ones on which they depend, are historically the last to understand the changes that are really going on among the people they are trying to govern, preserve, and protect. They can, if enlightened, make reforms. They seldom, if ever, can change basic injustices or keep pace with the changes taking place in their people.

The spiritual unrest is real. Like a stormy ocean, it heaves up waves of teachers, prophets, preachers, and saviors. Some but not many may be saints. Some are rogues for sure. It is too soon to tell for most. But all of them are aware that there is a great spiritual unrest, pregnant with possibility for good or evil, and that they might have a part in new forms and expressions of human meaning and destiny eventually emerging from this sea of unrest.

HUMAN SELF-AWARENESS

I will venture the guess that increasing awareness of the human potential will turn out to be the most important discovery of the 20th century and, indeed, of many centuries before it. It is this awareness that prompts the proliferation of saints and saviors, mystery religions, meditation cults, and self-help programs that are increasingly engaging the attention of those who seek personal growth. The phrase "the human potential" covers a wide range of human activities—some eccentric, some as yet largely esoteric, some wicked and fraudulent, some full of promise of new truth and human transformation. The essence of this discovery is that powers and resources are available to the ordinary human being from within his own personality or from the intellectual and spiritual world around him and are capable of helping him transform his life, enlarge his powers, and realize new dimensions of his human condition. A whole new world now waits to be explored and used for human good or evil. The situation is not unlike the moments when the first explorers stood on the peripheral islands and coasts of the Americas with little or no notion, or at times a mistaken idea, of where they were and what lay ahead.

We are aware of powers and resources only dimly perceived until now: a few saints, artists, wise men, and some whose names will never be known to history. The exploration and charting of this inner space is just starting; and we who are alive today, especially in the younger generation, are or can be the witnesses and participants in humanity's greatest adventure so far.

Looking back over the 20th century, we find a few intrepid explorers who have pointed out the dimensions of the discovery. William James, in his landmark study, *The Varieties of Religious Experience*, concludes that our life is "continuous with a wider self through which saving experiences come." Some of us were fortunate enough to have college philosophy teachers such as Rufus M. Jones and Douglas V. Steere to introduce them to the writings of the Christian mystics of the Middle Ages, together with the insights of Quakers into silence, meditation, and prayer. The works of Aldous Huxley, Gerald Heard, Joseph Campbell, F. S. C. Northrup, and other writers showed that the idea of the human potential was a universal idea rooted in all the great religions and their disciplines of meditation. Hermann Hesse in literature, together with poets like Wordsworth and nature observers like Thoreau, showed that the natural world could be a path to the understanding of the human potential. Psychologists such as Carl Jung, Gordon Allport, and more recently Carl Rogers, Abraham Maslow, and others showed the human potential in unexplored areas of the psyche. The interpreters of Zen like Alan Watts, D. T. Suzuki added another dimension to the search. J. B. Rhine's studies of ESP and related phenomena came at the problem from a different angle. A few books stand out as illuminating guides: Hesse's *Siddhartha*, Huxley's *The Perennial Philosophy*, Campbell's *The Masks of God*, Jung's *Memories, Dreams, Reflections.*

But all the explorations so far are in the early stages— suggestive, like the shores of the New World, of who knows what possibilities. Whoever explores here must therefore walk carefully and critically among the various paths that are being offered today. The first equipment for the journey is a set of standards for selection between true and false, right and wrong, authentic growth and self-deception.

SOME STANDARDS FOR JUDGMENT

Motive is of first importance. The great saints and teachers of a humane and spiritual way of life have been single-mindedly concerned with following the truth that they have found and helping others to see it and follow it, too. So far as personal gain, power, and number of adherents have been concerned, they have been quite disinterested. If the ordinary person wanted to follow, he could—provided he could meet the high standards they set. It is hard to judge motives, but purity of heart and strength of purpose are difficult to hide. They are rare, and they stand out among the more common and self-serving purposes of organizational work, fund raising, promotion, and the kind of evangelism based on numbers so frequently seen in the mass revival movements of our time. If you find that the leaders of the movement are very busy adding up the score of converts and pressing them into the organizational mold, beware.

Authoritarianism is an all too common characteristic of many movements in our time. It exists in government, business, labor unions, education, churches, the professions, and the family, in varying degrees. It can be identified wherever the attitude of the leadership toward criticism and questioning is that people must take the truth as the leaders provide it because the leaders say so. Wherever claims of supernatural authority are made or wherever the leader declares his own infallibility, watch out. Authority in sane and constructive religious or intellectual movements is based on knowledge and persuasion, but not knowledge and persuasion that cannot be questioned. Leaders and teachers always have the duty of explaining the truth they see in terms that thoughtful people can understand. Thus, leadership in an authentic religious movement is derived from the understanding and consent of those who are being led, and they retain their right to ask questions all along the way. Leadership is a two-way affair—up from the bottom, down from the top. If a group seems to have only one way—authority from the top down—be on your guard.

Secrecy is another danger sign in a movement that seeks to spread religious truth or promote personal growth. If the prospective disciple is led on by the promise of special secret knowledge to be revealed after he has reached a certain stage of loyalty, payment of money, or both, watch out. The deepest truths may be rare and difficult to achieve, but they are freely available to all who will seek. Jesus said, "Ask and it shall be given you, seek and you shall find, knock and it shall be opened." That is a valid guide for seekers after spiritual truth or personal growth. The role of a leader or teacher is not to guard a hidden truth or symbol, but to guide the seeker in making his own investigation and his own search. The secret is that there is no secret, although a difficult, exacting knowledge exists that a conscientious teacher can help us to attain. The gullible persist in believing that there is some hidden knowledge that solves all problems and makes fulfillment easy and swift. There is no such thing.

Social concern is a characteristic of fully developed religious faith and of mature personal growth. Religious and personal growth movements often begin with the development of the individual and the effort to liberate him from fear and hate so that he may reach his highest potential. But they should continue in the effort to direct his attention to the communities he belongs to and the importance of playing a constructive and loving role within each one of them. A person belongs to many communities: family, church, city, state, nation, and world, with many sub-groups under other headings. Genuine religious and personal growth is reflected in responsible membership and participation in these groups. If a religious group or a system of personal growth shows no interest and concern for the expressions of social justice, racial equality, civil liberties, humane law, and peaceful progress toward world order, insisting that all growth must start with the individual, beware. This is one of the great oversimplifications used by those who do not want social change and fear the revolution that enlightened social ethics will bring. To prevent change, they enlist religion and systems of personal growth on their side. It is also the point of greatest difference between philosophies of East and West. The West, for all its ethical dilemmas and failures, has been solidly based on the conviction that the transformed person shows the depth and sincerity of his transformation by his concern for social justice. Enlightened love of self and neighbor, and of ultimate values, all go together. The East traditionally seeks release of the self from desire. The East has turned in recent decades to Western methods of social development, but the systems of spiritual discipline imported from Eastern religions and philosophies tend to confine themselves mostly to personal growth. This emphasis is an important corrective to the West's concern with external things, but it should not be taken as a substitute for a healthy, active social conscience. The mature and fulfilled person cares about both his own growth and the human communities of which he is a part and on which he depends for the essentials of life and for warmth and moral support in his own life. Few of us live to ourselves alone; few of us want to. A philosophy of personal growth that does not require a social conscience should be regarded with some suspicion.

Unrelieved solemnity is a danger sign in any movement or teaching. It is possible to take life seriously without taking it so heavily that one is unable to smile at its ironies and laugh at its occasional foolishness. Humor reflects the ability of a person to look at himself and find amusement in his lapses and the ridiculous situations in which he sometimes finds himself.

A sense of humor suggests the presence of sanity, objectivity, and that awareness of human frailty that sympathizes rather than condemns. Individuals and movements that lack humor lack the ability to see themselves as they really are and hence the ability to see others as they really are. If there is no capacity to smile and laugh with kindness, something essential is missing.

These warnings may seem negative, but they are offered in the conviction that the basic concerns of enlightened religion and growth toward personal maturity are the same: the encouragement of people who are committed to the realization of the highest powers and the most ethical attitudes within themselves, and the application of those values to the communities to which they belong. Our basic values find their clearest expression or lack of expression in human relationships, and in growth of the highest virtues of wisdom and love. These, in their manifold forms and expressions, are the ends we seek when we try to discover the human potential and apply it to personal and social life.

Five Ways of Growth

Now we have cleared the ground for a look at some of the positive ways of helping the individual discover his own potential and setting his powers free to grow toward personal and social maturity.

The various manifestations of religion and self-help systems in our time can be classified under five basic headings, summarized here so that the reader can find his way among the varied groups that appeal for his interest, support, and loyalty.

Establishment churches and religions—Catholic, Protestant, and Jewish. These are the middle-of-the-road denominations that have been around for centuries in the Western world.

They meet regularly for worship and social activity. There is almost always a ritualistic service, fully developed in such churches as the Roman Catholic, Anglican, and Lutheran bodies, as well as in Orthodox and Conservative Judaism. There are sacred books; daily, weekly, and seasonal liturgies; highly trained priesthood or ministry. These elements appear in simpler form even in the so-called non-liturgical churches, where religious custom, even if it is largely didactic rather than symbolic, has achieved great authority through constant use.

We should not undervalue the importance of the established churches and synagogues. In spite of the fact that habit and common usage have reduced the vitality of many affirmations and commitments made in them, they still have a considerable power of survival. The traditional churches are constantly pronounced to be moribund and unable to meet the human need. They often seem so: they lack imagination, spontaneity, and the capacity to experiment and change with new insights. But they do change, although slowly, and these changes can be perceived if they are measured in decades and generations rather than months and years. Their very slowness to change may be a stabilizing influence that enables many people to find strength and a sense of direction in them. The established churches are admittedly conservative forces, and they seem too often to suffer from intellectual and spiritual inertia. But they provide a kind of balance that is essential to orderly growth and change, and they are there for weary pilgrims and explorers to come back to when they feel the need of returning and rest.

Another aspect of established churches—not so healthy and supportive of religious growth—is the tendency of the more successful ones, in terms of money, buildings, and popular following, to make something divine out of their success. Probably nothing in established churches has sent more religious seekers away hungry and disillusioned than the gospel of success. Smooth adjustment to a sick society is not a remedy for anybody's deep spiritual needs.

But on balance we should not dismiss the established religious institutions as hopeless. They have great value and meaning in spite of their limitations. They will be around when most of the new mystery religions, cults of salvation, and psychological therapies have been forgotten.

Efforts to revive the old faith in its ancient form. These seem to be primarily Protestant in source and expression. Catholicism and Judaism change, while persisting in the denial of change. That very fact provides a kind of continuity. Revivalism has been a steady feature of many Protestant groups. The old faith as taught in the Bible is always falling into decay and then being revived. The Reverend Billy Graham is no doubt the foremost revivalist of our time, but there are many others. Thousands have been attracted by the gospel presented with individual fervor, plus all the paraphernalia of modern promotion and communication. It can be a very exciting experience, even for those who do not make a "decision for Christ," to sit in a vast multitude and feel the power of the preacher's spoken word, the sentiment of the songs, and the mass hypnosis of a praying crowd.

Yet efforts to turn back the religious clock are not likely to accomplish much in the way of increasing awareness of religious values. They provide the feeling of renewal without the expansion of insight and consciousness that make it real. The kindest thing we can say about the new revivalism is that it does not seem very different from the old revivalism. We may hope it does no great harm. It is hard to see how it can do much good to the individual, since what is demanded of him is not searching or enlargement of his consciousness, but self-surrendering and acceptance of guidance from a supernatural power somewhere outside himself. Revivals will continue to be with us, but we shall look to them in vain for the religious personal growth for which so many hunger.

New Religions. One example will suffice, that of Sun Myung Moon and his Unification Church. The Reverend Mr. Moon brings from Korea both a highly successful business experience and an exotic gospel made up of revelations received by him and now being taught to his disciples, who are also his missionaries. The central teachings are derived from Christianity, but there are strange elements of Eastern mysticism and anti-communism. Jesus is presented as a savior who failed. A new Christ is now expected. He is not precisely identified, but according to the teaching, he was born in Korea in 1920. The Unification Church claims a worldwide membership of several million, mainly from Korea and Japan, but the United States is the new mission field. The church now claims a following here of many thousands. It is taking in millions of dollars a year in contributions and supports numerous training and fund-raising centers where people, mostly the young, learn to become missionaries. There is increasing evidence of compulsory tactics in some of the centers. Authoritarianism seems to be built into the organization at every level. Doubtless many of the converts have come willingly to the new faith, but it has proved more difficult for those who want to leave to do so peacefully. There even exists a Moon "alumni association" of embittered young people and their parents and friends.

Systems of Meditation.   The best known of these currently is Transcendental Meditation, the movement created by Maharishi Mahesh Yogi, and known popularly as TM. This movement began in India, but it has been westernized and is now offered as a means of achieving greater awareness, relaxation, personal growth, and increased productivity. TM has a number of centers in the United States, a college in Iowa, and a carefully planned system for spreading its teaching across the world. Its adherents are drawn from every age group and walk of life. Commendably, its leader, Maharishi, and his followers have been quite willing, even eager, to submit the results of their system to scientific study. Dr. Herbert Benson of the Harvard Medical School, in his book *The Relaxation Response*, documents the undeniable capacity of the TM system to achieve such physical results as the lowering of blood pressure and pulse; reduction of tension, oxygen consumption, metabolism rate; and the consequent improvement of the sense of well-being and productivity for those who practice meditation regularly. They are also better able to deal with such addictions as alcohol, tobacco, and drugs; and they discover new possibilities within themselves.

TM seems unable to decide whether or not it is a religion. It claims not to be one, since it insists that people of all faiths or of none can learn and derive benefit from its technique of meditation. At the same time, TM seems to create within its adherent something of loyalty and commitment characteristic of strong religious feelings. Its insistence on the secrecy of the mantras given by its teachers as aids of meditation and its active missionary spirit give it a religious quality. This issue will present itself increasingly as TM grows in the United States and confronts the constitutional separation of church and state.

There are currently many other ways of meditation that are being offered. The major religions of Catholic and Protestant Christianity, Judaism, Islam, and Buddhism all have numerous methods that may be followed. The range of Christian meditation stretches from the highly organized systems of Catholicism to the simple openness of Quakerism. The Sufi sect of Islam offers a literature and a path for the serious seeker. Zen meditation is taught in a number of teaching centers in America and may be studied in various forms. There are other Buddhist sects such as the "Pure Land" Buddhist church, the Tendai, the Nichiren, the Kegon sects, and numerous others. Hinduism is represented in the Ramakrishna Society, which has long been established in America. In addition, one can find in meditation guides like Lawrence LeShan's *How to Meditate* a number of scientific-psychological approaches to meditation that may be more acceptable to the Western mind. In fact, the seeker in this field will be tempted to spend too much time examining the possibilities before choosing and following a specific way for his own growth. The temptation to become a dilettante is strong and must be resisted with the reflection that there are many paths to essentially the same truths in this little-known region.

Systems of therapy.   Groups of this kind do not have the sense of membership common to the religious or quasi-religious groups, although certain therapies have at times generated considerable fervor in their adherents. The therapies are directed by persons with some professional standing— psychiatrists, psychologists, clergy, and other experts—who have gone to great pains to get specialized knowledge of the particular therapy they practice. They believe deeply, but tend to avoid the messianic emphasis, and they offer various approaches to the achievement of personal health and wholeness, most of which have clear if sometimes partial validity. Their errors, if they are errors, come when their proponents tend to apply one specialized therapy to all needs and conditions. This is a common mistake and familiar in religious history. Once somebody begins to insist that his part of the truth is the whole truth and hence all that needs to be known, he is involved in a heresy or, much worse, an idolatry. He is also involved in the intellectual error of confusing the part with the whole.

Among the therapies in this group, and this is not an exhaustive list, are Transactional Analysis, Gestalt, Psychodrama, Encounter Therapy, and many others. They become dangerous only when they become cults and ends in themselves, rather than aids to the realization of deeper consciousness and heightened awareness of reality.

Now we are ready to look at some standards by which we can judge the authenticity of the array of movements covered in these five categories.

2

on Theory

ᵪ some current teachers serious-
ıt discovery, like television or the
ather, one of the great common
ꜱ of all of the world's religions,
ıs to the most complex and highly
ior contemplation. Meditation is
ᵻct of attention will vary: a god, an
ion, a way of life, a spiritual ground
ᵤₑₛₜ, es silence, the peace beyond all
thought, all or nothingness, an end to contradictions and verbal
symbols.

The perennial philosophy is the name given by Aldous Huxley to the basic theory behind all meditative processes. He
made it the title of an anthology with interpretative comments
which remains one of the best introductions to the field of
mysticism. The essence of the perennial philosophy is that
there exists in all cultures and religions an awareness of the
ground of all being, together with the experiences of some who
have realized by way of meditation and contemplation (sometimes the way is called prayer) their identity with this ground
and have developed an on-going relationship to it that perme-
ated their whole lives. Sometimes, as in Jewish, Christian, and
Islamic mysticism, the ground has been experienced as transcendent spiritual reality, God who exists and dwells on a
different order of being from the human mind and spirit but

whose transcendent being can be experienced by mere humans because there is "that of God" in each person. Sometimes, as in some expressions of Buddhism, Hinduism, and Taoism, as well as in psychologically and scientifically oriented experience, the ground is seen to be an extension of the consciousness of the individual mind, an increase in awareness, a realization that one is part of a larger natural and human consciousness. This sense of relationship can be deepened and illuminated through regular meditation, and the results of this effort are increased satisfaction in living, better use of one's mind and body, and a deeper realization of what we now call "the human potential."

The perennial philosophy is both natural and supernatural, humanistic and theistic, a part of ordinary experience and something that transcends ordinary experience. These differences are products of the various religions and cultures through which it has been expressed over the centuries. The individual approaching meditation should consider the perennial philosophy as the theoretical foundation of his search and choose from its amazing variety of expressions such statements and symbols as are most helpful to him. The point is that in meditation one is taking a practical path of growth, not a theoretical path of intellectualizing and precise definition. One follows the path that seems most natural, confident that whether he approaches the ground of being over the natural, the supernatural, the theistic, the humanistic, the positive, the negative, the active, or the passive route is not as important as persistence in the way he has chosen, since all ways of strengthening our awareness of the depths within our own minds and spirits will eventually lead us to the ground of all being. Evelyn Underhill in *The Golden Sequence* has described the situation in the figure of a wheel. We imagine ourselves at the start somewhere on the circumference, the rim, of a great wheel. We may be at the Christian position or that of some other religion. But there are also an agnostic position, a scientific position, even a skeptical "show me if you can" position. Each one of these positions is represented by a spoke of the wheel. The only requirement is that the seeker beginning at the circumference from his own position make a serious, patient effort to move along his spoke toward the center, the hub of the wheel, which is the ground of being. Starting from any given point on the circumference and moving toward the center, it comes about that the nearer one is to the center the nearer one is to all the other seekers on all the other spokes of the wheel. This accounts for the empirical fact that the mathematician or physicist can recognize what the mystic is talking about. The theist Christian or Jew can appreciate and learn from what the Zen Buddhist is saying or experiencing. We are dealing here with one of humanity's universal quests and experiences. It may well be as important and necessary a characteristic of the human creature as the needs for food, sex, and love. As the beginning meditator makes his way through the literature and the varied symbols of meditation, he should keep the image of the wheel in mind. It will help him to realize that what seems strange to him may not be on closer understanding so strange at all. It may simply be another way of expressing what he is finding along his way.

Some Basic Assumptions

Whatever the object of meditation, the methods used will be much the same, at least at the start. However, there are certain distinctions among various meditative paths that the beginning meditator should keep in mind as a means of clarifying his own thought. The word "transcendental" is common in meditative literature, particularly recently. We may ask what is to be transcended. Is the meditation directed toward an objective reality outside the self, like God or the spiritual realm, or is the meditation transcendental in the sense that through this process the meditator touches deeper levels of being within his own consciousness? Or is the meditation transcendental in the sense that the meditator is in touch with a larger self, but not a god, derived from the collective experience and wisdom of the race, perhaps something like Jung's collective unconscious? All of these are possibilities. In Christianity, Judaism, and Islam the object of meditation may be union with the godhead, the realization that each soul is part of the eternal life of God, the all in all. But the meditator, not being a theist, may still feel participation in a larger life simply by realizing this identity with levels of awareness in his own being which he has not hitherto discovered. There is an important difference between, on the one hand, perceiving things and events differently because the self has reached new levels of understanding through meditation and, on the other hand, the perception of different things and events because the self has penetrated beneath the level of the merely human and personal to the depths as a being united with, yet separate from the individual. The first assumption suggests a one-level world where the natural includes all phenomena that human beings can be aware of, including those spiritual perceptions that we used to call divine and supernatural. It assumes that our ordinary life becomes, at its deepest levels, one with the larger life of all humanity and all nature. Whatever gods there be will be felt and understood as part of the natural world and natural truth. As Santayana said, "There is only one world, the natural world, and only one truth about it: but this world has a spiritual life in it which looks not to another world but to the beauty and perfection that this world suggests, approaches, and misses."[1]

A second assumption suggests the existence and presence of the transcendent god who is apart from human beings, yet one with them at the deepest levels of consciousness. Here the end of meditation is union with God. The assumption will, of course, be more palatable to those who have been schooled in traditional religious circles and feel at home with the symbols of divinity.

A third assumption, which is characteristic of Zen and of Buddhism generally, as well as of the most advanced mystics of all religions, is that the ultimate quality is beyond all rational and theoretical distinctions. Only as we escape from the "rational trap" do we begin to approach spiritual reality. This

assumption is the hardest for the Western mind to comprehend. Most of us are used to the idea of finding and formulating
clear definitions of everything. We think that if we have expressed a definition of something, we understand it. In short,
we confuse words with experience and reality. Thus the techniques of meditation taught in Zen are essentially an assault on
the rational process. They are calculated to show how futile and
foolish it is to try to catch reality in a verbal trap. The Zen
master's nonsensical answers to his students' questions, the
koans that mock rationality, the unpredictable outbursts of
laughter, anger, or ridicule are all designed to teach the earnest seeker after truth that as long as he is trying to catch truth
in a definition he is doomed to frustration. Only when he leaves
reason behind and becomes empty, open, not even expectant,
will he begin to approach reality; and then, if he tries to seize it,
it will elude him.

The Western mind can find room for Santayana's one natural
world with only one truth about it within its rationalistic,
scientific tradition. It can still relate to the second—the idea of
union with God—through its traditional religious past. It takes
a tremendous effort, a revolutionary turnabout, for the Western mind to grasp Zen, much less feel at home within its style of
thought and feeling. Some have been able to do so. Alan Watts
is a notable example of one who not only did so but could
explain the process in vivid language to persons still thinking
out of the forms of Western thought.

The crucial question is how much time and effort should
those of us who are incorrigibly Western in our attitudes of
thought and feeling be ready to spend on an effort at total
reconstruction. It would seem wiser perhaps to do our own
thing in our own way in meditation, using what we can of
Eastern wisdom and technique, but not thinking of ourselves
as second-class meditators because we are not equal to the
strenuous demands of Zen and cannot achieve satori or nirvana. The Western tradition of meditation is rich in its own right,
and many of the best aspects of Eastern spirituality can be
adapted to our purposes without violation of their essential

spirit. Nowhere are East and West closer than in the field of meditation. For each spiritual tradition has sought union with the ground of being, using its own special forms and symbols, some of which are interchangeable while others are not.

READINESS

Fortunately, the individual seeking to follow the meditative path need not make a decision in advance about the underlying suppositions of the way. In fact, it is better if he does not do so. For if he does enter into meditation with a set of prior convictions and assumptions, he will demand that they be validated in his meditative efforts. But since meditation is essentially the effort to enter into great areas of hitherto unknown experience within and beyond the individual's unconscious mind, efforts to impress some dogmatic system of belief upon what is discovered are almost certain to be disappointing. It is better to proceed with an open mind, ready to accept and ponder what comes, than to insist on shaping what comes in accordance with one's preconceived ideas. The point is well made in a famous letter written by the great biologist T. H. Huxley to his friend the writer Charles Kingsley. Kingsley had written Huxley a letter of Christian sympathy on the occasion of the death of Huxley's ten-year-old son. He had expressed the hope that Huxley, a confirmed agnostic, might be able to accept the Christian doctrine of resurrection and find comfort in it. Huxley replied that, while he appreciated Kingsley's concern, he could not accept this faith. He continued:

> But the longer I live, the more obvious it is to me that the most sacred act of a man's life is to say and to feel, "I believe such and such to be true." All the greatest rewards and the heaviest penalties of existence cling about that act. . . . Science seems to me to teach in the highest and strongest manner the great truth which is embodied in the Christian conception of entire surrender to the will of God. Sit down before fact as a little child, be prepared to

give up every preconceived action, follow humbly wherever and to whatever abysses Nature leads, or you shall learn nothing. I have only begun to learn content and peace of mind since I have resolved at all risks to do this.[2]

That is the right mood in which to enter meditation: a readiness to accept what comes, a patient expectancy of discovery without a preconceived notion of what is to be discovered. When one takes a bath, one strips naked to prepare for the cleansing and bracing encounter with fresh water. When one enters meditation, one is ready to be cleansed, braced, renewed, without demanding to know in advance just how it will happen. The readiness is all.

Theoretical assumptions are best arrived at through experience rather than in advance of it. That is the basic empirical truth. Those who follow the meditative path need not be Christians, Jews, Buddhists, or anything else. They need not be theists, humanists, agnostics, either. They can be any or all of these. What they must be is open and ready to discover and learn from their own experience. The ultimate questions of existence—creation, divinity, human nature, good and evil, immortality of the soul—need not be answered in advance. It is better if they are not. The great spiritual teachers have been aware of this fact. They have stressed the way rather than the beliefs about ultimate reality. When people came to Jesus with these unanswerable questions, he said in effect, "Never mind. Follow me." And the Buddha pointed to the eight-fold path, indicating that his disciples should follow those steps rather than concern themselves over unanswerable questions. In short, philosophical truth comes out of experience, not the other way around.

This process of going forward without knowing the answers may be hard for us to accept until we realize that this is the way all life is lived most of the time. Only very rarely do human beings proceed with certainty; and then, more often than not, they are disappointed because new elements of experience appear and upset their expectations. Most life is lived on the basis of a little knowledge and a lot of hope and trust. The development of a theory of the meaning of what you do comes later. Philosophy follows life.

There is a mythical old lady who, when asked what she thought about some urgent matter, replied, "Think? How do I know what I think until I hear what I'm going to say?" She was not empty-headed, just realistic.

The essential thing in meditation is the realization that the depths of possibility within the self, within all selves, and within the natural creation are unexplored but available to the open mind and the trusting heart.

COMING HOME

Lawrence LeShan, in his excellent book, *How to Meditate: A Guide to Self-Discovery*, suggests another aspect of meditation theory that may be helpful. He describes a meeting of scientists where the small group present were asked why they meditated. After a number had given answers that seemed to miss the mark, one ventured the statement that it was "like coming home."[3] This answer seemed to satisfy all present, and nothing further needed to be said. The idea of homecoming is a theme that exerts a universal allurement for human beings from every religion and culture. Plato's theory of ideas suggests the prior existence of a world of perfect forms, of which the present world of experience is only an imperfect copy. Human beings, it is said, bring into their immediate search for knowledge and meaning an awareness of an earlier existence where they were aware of a fuller and more perfect life. The followers of Plato through the centuries have repeated this theme. One of the most beautiful and touching expressions of it is Wordsworth's "Ode on the Intimations of Immortality."

> Our birth is but a sleep and a forgetting:
> The Soul that rises with us, our life's Star,
>   Hath had elsewhere its setting,

And cometh from afar:
Not in entire forgetfulness,
And not in utter nakedness,
But trailing clouds of glory do we come
From God, who is our home. . . .

Hence in a season of calm weather
Though inland far we be,
Our Souls have sight of that immortal sea
Which brought us hither,
Can in a moment travel thither,
And see the Children sport upon the shore,
And hear the mighty waters rolling evermore.[4]"

The doctrine of recollection here stated says that we once shared in a larger life, that we have vague memories of it, and that "in a season of calm weather," perhaps in a time of meditation, we can recapture something of what we once knew.

Jesus went even further and suggested in the famous parable of the Prodigal Son that when we "come to ourselves" we can leave an arid and half-awake life behind and return to the forgiveness of welcome in the heavenly Father. Whatever doctrines or symbols we use to describe it, the impulses that lead us to meditation are likely to be an uneasy awareness that life is moving on and we are missing something that we once knew or long to have, and that this precious something can be recovered or found if we will begin to search. There is also the premonition that when we do find the way it will lead us to something like home, a place or a condition where we feel happy and secure in ourselves, close to others around us, and open to a larger life in which we always dimly felt we had a part. Robert Frost wrote in "The Death of the Hired Man," "Home is the place where, when you have to go there, they have to take you in."[5] The current concern with meditation is surely part of the profound homesickness of modern man for a world in which he can be himself at his best, reaching out to others at their best. This homesickness cannot be dismissed as regressive. It is an awareness of a larger life to which we are related but with which we rarely get in touch. Meditation is the way we get in touch with that life. This will serve as a working definition. Now we are ready to think about what to do in meditation itself.

3

What To Do

The Secret

We have now examined the perennial philosophy as the universal theory behind the process of meditation and noticed that each of us has a need and a longing to realize and develop our connectedness with the ground of being. This we do through the discipline of meditation. There is also, as Dr. Herbert Benson and others have shown through their research, a physiological ground for meditation. Meditation not only opens channels of communication with the ground of being; it also opens channels of communication to the body and its vital functions such as breathing, heartbeat, blood pressure, nervous tensions, etc. The mental and spiritual activity of meditation has real and measurable effects upon the rest of the organism. Dr. Benson calls these effects "the relaxation response." There are many other names that might be given them: relief from stress, ordering of the mind and emotions, reinforcement of personal strength and sense of direction, cleansing of the senses, and clarification of the mind. These are some of the values that are open and achievable at the price of some quiet and persistent discipline of the body and the mind. Dr. Benson's book is directed primarily at those who labor under great stress, and it offers them an alternative to constant tension and weariness. But whoever you are and whatever you do, the great exponents of the perennial philosophy affirm that meditation will help you become a more centered and ordered person. Whatever you have to cope with you will be able to cope with better for having spent some time and effort at the meditative task. In short, meditation is important because it will help you become more controlled, more calm, and more aware of your own life, the lives of others, and the ongoing life of the whole natural world around you. You will be wider awake and hence able to enjoy life more. You will be stronger personally and hence better able to meet whatever difficulties and sufferings confront you. These are quite specific and very desirable promises. How do we go about realizing them?

Writers on meditation like Dr. Benson, Dr. LeShan, the Maharishi, Thomas Merton, Alan Watts, and others add little to the basic requirements, except to put them in a setting that is acceptable to the contemporary mind. I am about to reveal to you the secret of meditation absolutely free: The secret is that there is no secret. The basic requirements have been known for centuries. Here they are:

1. To create an opportunity for quietness.
2. To find the right time and place.
3. To find the means of cleansing your mind and your emotions of extraneous, irrelevant thoughts and feelings so that you are open to receive the deeper wisdom that comes from the ground of being.
4. To persist at the task without expecting miracles or quick results.
5. To let the renewed strength and deepened insight that come to you flow out through you into the world around you, thus improving your own enjoyment of life, deepening your own human relations, and replenishing your own sense of participation and usefulness in the human adventure.

GUIDELINES

We shall begin at the beginning. We must create an opportunity for quietness. This is not always easy to do, but it is not impossible. None of us is so busy that there is no time for a half hour when we are alone and able to be quiet, reasonably free from interruption, and disposed to spend that time not on busy work, but on the effort to collect ourselves and explore the depths of our own being. Perhaps the hardest thing is the deliberate decision to do it and to tell those who are concerned that you want to be alone, that you would prefer not to be interrupted, and that the purpose of this time of quietness is to permit you to meditate. We feel shy about this kind of revelation, as if the desire to meditate were something to be ashamed of, a revelation of inner weakness. On the contrary, it is a revelation of inner strength, or at least of the need for strength. A person who frankly admits that he needs to grow in order to become whole is not weak; he is beginning to be strong. He is not sick; he is beginning to be well. Hence, I think the decision to meditate should be an explicit one that is shared with somebody who knows and loves you, if that person is in any way to be affected by it. The sharing of the decision shows that you take the other person seriously and that you take the decision seriously yourself. We have all done a lot of things that we needed to do and did not feel like doing at the time because we quietly promised ourselves and somebody else that we would do them. The sharing with somebody you love of your promise to yourself to meditate will help you to keep that promise and confirm the love and trust between you and that other person. In asking that person to respect this deep need in you, you are expressing your knowledge of and gratefulness for that person's love for you.

So now you are ready to start. What will you do? Sit down comfortably in a place where your senses and your mind can be relatively at peace. I know that people can learn to meditate in taxis, buses, trains, airplanes, crowded stations, or theatres. But if you do not have to add the inevitable difficulties and distractions, why do so? Most places where people live have a spot where a person can sit quietly with the knowledge and cooperation of others who live there. Do not choose a place with too many distractions—too busy a view of the outside world, too cluttered a desk or table. I found that I had to pick up my desk before I could sit in front of it for meditation, but I also found that having it in order with my few little tokens and keepsakes arranged in their right places was a great help. The ordered desk can suggest the ordered life.

There are many suggestions as to position. Some people feel that meditation is impossible without getting into the lotus position. This requirement would exclude a great many people, including me and most Westerners over thirty. Others have insisted that kneeling was essential, but kneeling seems to belong to a world most of us have left behind. Our beliefs in God, if we have any, do not envisage him as an Oriental potentate sitting on a throne while his subjects kneel or prostrate themselves before him. The best thing is to get a position that is comfortable and natural. The trouble with lying down is that it may get too comfortable and you will go to sleep. The trouble with standing up is that it may grow uncomfortable to stand still, and moving about too much will be distracting. On the whole, for people in our society, sitting in a comfortable chair is probably the best.

While it is good to have a regular time for meditation, it is best to make that time somewhat flexible. For instance, if it is eight o'clock and you must be somewhere at eight-thirty, you will put yourself under a deadline, and that will bother you. Put some space around your meditation island, so that if you are a few minutes late in starting, or interrupted, or a few minutes late in ending, you need not feel pressed. To be sure of a half hour, set forty minutes aside. A psychiatrist once told me that the famous fifty-minute hour was not a means of cheating the patient, nor solely a device to let the doctor go to the bathroom, but a means of letting the doctor recover from one encounter and prepare himself for the next one.

You are now seated wherever you have chosen to sit. Close your eyes, relax your muscles, let your hands rest quietly in your lap. You are ready to begin. The ancient Hindu and Buddhist methods call for quiet, regular breathing and an awareness of breathing as the basic bodily rhythm that it is. We are seldom aware of our breathing unless it is too fast from some exertion or deliberately made deep and slow by a concentrated effort. Be conscious of the steady, rhythmic in-and-out process of breathing. Dr. Benson and Dr. LeShan, following the yogis and the Zen teachers, suggest that the way to become quietly conscious of breathing is to count slowly in and out. I have found this to be a good idea. You can do it almost unconsciously, and it helps you to move along through time. By the way, many people have found that lying down and breathing in the way I have described is a fine way to fall asleep. If that happens while you are trying to meditate, it means that your bodily position is a little too relaxed. The meditative state of consciousness is neither sleeping nor waking nor dreaming, but a separate state in itself.

We now come to the central problem in meditation: how to close off the senses, empty the mind of extraneous material, and open its channels to receive the quietness and sense of peace that come through from the ground of being. Some schools of thought, notably the Rinzai Zen school, favor the use of a *koan* or nonsense statement or question that absorbs the meditator's attention completely to the exclusion of all else, baffles his reasoning faculties, and yields only in a swift moment of insight. Another Zen school, the Soto sect, insists that the mind must be made completely vacant, perhaps the hardest thing in the world to do. Most Christian, Jewish, and Islamic-Sufi schools say that, while the goal of meditation may be simple openness and receptiveness, one must start with some mental images or verbal statements that enlist the meditator's attention. One can think of a great many simple sentences that might open the way. They come from religion, poetry, literature, even one's own imagination. For example, turn over in your mind a statement like, "Now abide faith, hope, love, these three, and the greatest of these is love," and you will have a jewel of meditation that will occupy you for a long time. Or try Keats's "Beauty is truth, truth beauty—That is all ye know on earth and all ye need to know." Or try Thoreau's, "There is more day yet to dawn. The sun is but a morning star." Try any simple statement, the briefer the better, that says something important to you and is deeply implanted in your memory. Let the statement rest in your mind.

Wander around it. Repeat it slowly. Look at it from various angles. Do not argue with it. Just try to find out what its possible meanings may be. There will be many that you have not realized before. Use the statement as an attention device. If you start to worry about some encounter that is coming up later, some job to be done, some difficulty to be met, put them aside quietly and return to the statement as if to say to each pressing concern, "All right, I'll take care of you in due time. Right now I'm meditating." You may find with some practice that you will break through your attention statement into a period of deep quietness in which you simply breathe and feel the openness and depths of your own mind as it is touched by surrounding depths. If that happens, and it will probably not happen very often, do not worry. Go with the flow. That is what meditation is all about: When the meditator stops thinking, speaking, feeling, and simply is, then he is ready to receive from the depths around and beneath him.

You may wish to use more elaborate systems of directed thought. Some of the Christian saints offer to lead us through various stages of the great parables of the New Testament into the farther reaches of meditation. Others, however, seem more like the Oriental mystics, in that they lead us away from images toward that emptiness of mind and spirit that is to be filled by the joy and grace of the divine being. Thus Eckhart writes:

> A man has many skins in himself, covering the depths of his heart. Man knows so many things; he does not know himself. Why, thirty or forty skins or hides, just like an ox's or a bear's, so thick and hard, cover the soul. Go into your own ground and learn to know yourself.[6]

I have included in a later chapter several sample patterns of meditation, some adapted to theistic use, some adapted to a more humanistic or scientific frame of mind. It should be remembered that in either case we are talking about the same process and the same reality. It is simply that some people speak a different language from others. Some speak "theistic," and some speak "humanistic." Neither term excludes the other.

Beginning with fifteen or twenty minutes a day, the individual may, if he wishes and finds the process rewarding, expand the time to thirty minutes or even more. It is probably best, if one has that much time, to break it into two periods, morning and evening. Some will find early morning before rising a good time for meditation. Others will find the time just before bedtime auspicious. These choices must be left to personal preference and convenience. The major point is to set up a steady, orderly process whereby one's mind is regularly opened to the vast depths around him, so that the state of meditation becomes a part of life as are waking, sleeping, dreaming, and other essential activities.

One should not seek or expect miraculous results. There will probably be none; and if there were, they would only be disconcerting. The masters of the spiritual life have been suspicious of easy ecstasy. It is beside the point, anyway, since the aim is to develop slowly a more collected mind and a steadier step through the ordinary tasks and experiences of life. Everyone who has had experience with meditation bears witness to the fact that there will be times of dryness and staleness as well as times of satisfaction. In either case, one is not to worry or be turned aside from the path, but rather one goes ahead steadily. When the fog comes into our little cove and covers the friendly gleam of the lighthouse flashing regularly every few seconds, we do not feel anxiety or despair. We know that the lighthouse is there. The light will be seen again as soon as the fog lifts. Meanwhile, there is nothing to be done about it except go ahead with the usual course of life. It is the same with dark times when our insight and understanding seem to fail. They will return, perhaps even deeper than they were before the darkness settled in.

We shall know what good our meditation does us not by any spectacular increase in wisdom or strength, but by the realization that from time to time some things that used to get us down no longer do so as much as they did. Or perhaps some desires that once owned us can now be controlled and used intelligently and moderately. Perhaps we sleep a little better or find that we feel less tired or can now look calmly and collectedly at some prospects that used to frighten us. It is best not to define in advance what the results of right meditation may be, since they will be different in individual cases. It is enough to say that the individual who meditates well and truly will find it worthwhile. It will become a part of his life as naturally as the other basic activities. He will learn the truth of the saint who said, "The less I pray, the worse it goes."

Meditation ought to lead to something practical. The greatest weakness of some of the modern systems is that they seem directed almost exclusively at helping people to enhance themselves, their own pleasure, their own effectiveness, even their own power and ambition. I think that something basic in meditation will be lost if we leave it at the point of self-satisfaction and self-fulfillment. We are not at our best when we live to ourselves alone; and we do, as Jesus suggested, find ourselves most truly when we have dared to forget ourselves in the service of something we value supremely. We are at our best when we are using the best of ourselves for some purpose greater than ourselves. In the soundest meditators there is an interesting and convincing alternation between meditation and action. They are not withdrawn from the world, but more intelligently and intensely involved in the world, because what they do is not mere reaction to outward pressures, but the expression of deep inward convictions and values.

Several years ago three management-level engineers at a GE nuclear research center in San Jose, California, resigned from their secure and well-paid positions in protest against the development of nuclear power as a "technological monster that threatens all future generations." They were joined by a federal official from the U.S. Nuclear Regulatory Commission, who resigned because his agency was telling the public that the nuclear plants were safe, when there was no scientific basis for saying that. These were principled acts, acts of conscience. They must have come from careful knowledge, serious consideration of the personal consequences, and a courageous decision to speak out on behalf of human life and a better future for all people. I do not know whether the scientists were meditators or not, but they must have done something akin to meditation before giving such clear expression to a hard and risky conviction. Their act has a ring of authenticity that is found only in deeply committed consciences. As one of their wives remarked, "When he broached the subject, my first thought was what about our security. Then I started thinking about the greatest kind of security—to do what you think is right."

I think we can predict that the current popular interest in meditation and related subjects will blossom and fade within a few years except among those who have found ways of giving simple, direct expression to their clarified minds and deepened awareness in efforts to affect some of the basic moral decisions confronting our society. These decisions relate to war and peace, justice and injustice, love and hate, truth and the lie in our national and international life. There may be very little we as individuals can do, but that little we must try to do if we are to keep our consciences clean in a historical period that seems to care very little about such quaint concerns. Yet in the long run I think that moral integrity will be a test, perhaps the ultimate test, of the depth and significance of one's personal search in meditation and self-development.

Douglas Steere makes the careful distinction between work and contemplation by pointing out that "work without contemplation is blind." That is, if we simply keep active without contemplation, our work soon becomes mere busy work, occupational therapy. Activity draws its meaning from the depths of our contemplation. But at the same time, "contemplation without work is dead." If we do nothing to give tangible, compassionate expression to our contemplation, then our inner life becomes dull and sterile. After all, how have we improved ourselves if we have not improved ourselves as members of the human family? Keeping meditation or contemplation and the ethical life of conscience and human concern together is a necessity for personal growth and fulfillment.

We have now set forth five guidelines for effective meditation. To summarize quickly:

1. Create an opportunity for quietness within your own life.
2. Select a time and place that suit your temperament and needs as well as the understanding of the people with whom you live.
3. Find an intellectual means of turning your attention steadily inward and keeping it there, as free as possible from distractions. Seek the ground of being in yourself.
4. Persist patiently. Do not expect miracles or quick results.
5. Find means of expressing your deepening awareness in simple, direct actions that improve human and natural relations.

The next chapter explores some of the possible patterns of meditation, in the hope that each person will find something he can work with and possibly be stimulated to create some patterns that are uniquely his own and hence more helpful than any that can be devised for him by others.

4

Ways of Meditating

In the previous chapter we suggested five guidelines or conditions essential to significant meditation. There are many ways of meditating. All of the major religions have developed them in wide proliferation. Some are very complex; some are quite simple. Some are very simple in appearance but very difficult in performance, because they are so demanding of human, emotional, and bodily discipline. Some are theological—theistic, pantheistic, atheistic, humanistic. Some are purely psychological. Because the goal of meditation is knowledge and experience of a non-rational kind, it is not easy to offer a clear, rational explanation of what it is all about. The person who achieves the goal: satori, nirvana, blessedness, the Buddha nature, union with God, peace, or whatever else he may call it, may often find himself quite unable to explain what he has found. He may smile or weep or say, "oh" or "ah"—all very perplexing and annoying to our concept-ridden minds.

Yet there are some means whereby people may move in the direction of this goal, which all religions and systems agree is so highly desirable, so beautiful, so self-validating that it needs no further explanation once it has been experienced or even glimpsed in the distant horizon of one's inner life. I have arranged these means under headings of the five senses and the ordinary communicators of conceptual thoughts—words—in the belief that however far we travel, we all start from the data that the five senses bring us and the connections and meanings of those data that appear as the rational mind sorts them out and puts them in words.

VISUAL IMAGES

Visual images and symbols are familiar in the drawing, painting, sculpture, pottery, jewelry, architecture, and related arts and crafts of every culture. Even the simplest and most primitive cultures have developed systems of meaning and communication based on pictures and symbols. The more highly developed cultures have created almost infinite elaborations and refinements in the effort to convey shades of meaning and varieties of form. Most obvious as the sources of meditation are the statues of gods, angels, animals, or men and women performing all kinds of functions believed to be characteristic of or illuminating to human beings. Some of the imagery is surpassingly beautiful, some of it pretty grim and bloody. Human life does contain both ecstasy and tragedy, and sometimes the two are closely intertwined. Images of Jesus, of the Virgin Mary and her child, of the angels, the apostles, the saints, the animals around the stable at Jesus' birth, and other holy beings are familiar in Christianity. They have their counterparts in other religions. The Hindu gods are numerous and appear in holy places as well as in the homes and personal shrines of devout believers. Although the Buddha did not teach belief in any god as a supreme being, he suffered the fate of other great teachers and was himself transformed into a god by his enthusiastic followers. Hence, his image appears wherever Buddhism has taken root in any of its hundreds of sects. There is a temple in Kyoto known as "the temple of the thousand Buddhas," where a thousand almost identical statues of the Buddha are arranged in three long rows in the great shed-like building. Since Mahayana Buddhism developed the idea of the Bodhisattva, one of a succession of many enlightened ones who have come to the world to manifest the universal compassion, images of these saviors are found in Buddhist shrines everywhere.

Other Buddhist pictures include the famous Zen series of the Ten Oxherding Pictures, which depict the man conquering his animal passions symbolized in the gradually diminishing figure of the ox, until at last the ox is no more, and in the end even the man is no more, since he has been absorbed into the universal consciousness. Millions of Christians still meditate and pray before pictures or images of Jesus, the Madonna, a saint, the stations of the cross, the crucifix, and other holy objects. Millions of Buddhists and Hindus meditate before statues of the Buddha or a particular god. Others find special significance in symbols like the cross, the crescent, the circle, the little curved lines that stand for yin and yang, the lotus, and many others. We are by no means liberated from visual symbols, although we may think we are. Almost everyone has a few small, rather personal objects which have particular significance because of some special experience connected with them.

The presence of such symbols is not to be ridiculed or condemned. Personally, I find having a few such symbols around me very reassuring and enlivening. My personal symbols recall for me events, relationships, travels, experiences that have enriched my life in one way or another. They help me return to those moments and enjoy them over again as I relive them. But they are not very helpful for meditation, since they evoke the personal, self-centered mood of memory and emotional involvement at a time when I want to be free of those feelings insofar as I can, so that my mind and heart are open and at rest. Meditation begins with the cleansing and emptying of the mind, rather than with the filling of it with stimuli, even the stimuli of happy memories and hopes. Hence, I would suggest that the beginning meditator go very slowly with the process of using visual symbols and images as aids to his meditation. Keep the mind free and open, hard as that may be.

It is said that in the Jewish temple in Jerusalem "the holy of holies" as it was called, the central point in the temple which was never visited by anyone except the high priest, and by him only once a year at the time of the High Holy Days, when he went there to carry vicariously the penitence of all Israel, was in fact a simple empty room, quite small and completely unadorned. It is probable that the center of the individual's being is a similar small room—empty, quiet, and unadorned. Judaism and Islam seem to be the only religions that have succeeded in preserving the sound insight that there should be no pictures or statues of the highest. God is spirit and therefore not the subject for pictorial treatment of any kind.

SOUND

Along with sight, sound is the other principal way in which impressions, ideas, feelings reach the mind. We shall be talking about words, sentences, and paragraphs in a subsequent section of this chapter. At the moment I am concerned with sound of a nonverbal kind: the sounds of nature and the sounds of civilization, as well as the sound of music, that most subtle and universal of the arts. For the most part, so far as the meditator is concerned, the sounds of nature, interesting and attractive as they may often be, are barriers rather than aids in the process of training the mind to pay attention to the inner life. Sounds that are part of the natural background—bird songs, the movement of water, the wind in the trees, the patter of rain—can all be absorbed into a kind of background for the meditator's attentiveness. But natural sounds do not keep pace with the flow of our minds. There are always abrupt changes and intrusions that destroy concentration—the squawk of a jay or a crow, the patter of rain that turns to a heavy shower, the crash of thunder—things like these do not help but hinder the effort to quiet the mind. They seem to command immediate attention and response. It is hard to sit still and let them flow around you. You are in the midst of them. The best you can do is treat them as for the most part benign interruptions and go on with your meditation.

The same may be said for music. Many untrained people think that music should be ideal for a background to meditation. But, at least in my experience, it is quite the opposite. I love music, and if it is around, it immediately engages my attention. I become interested in its form. I wonder who wrote it. If I know the music, I wait for its expected themes and patterns to unfold. If I do not know it, I listen carefully to see if I can discern the themes and patterns of sound. Either way, my meditative process loses out. With some humility I must admit that the best music for meditation may be something like Muzak, the inane, persistent background noise that has at least the value of demanding nothing from the mind and blotting out other harsher noises in the environment. This may be the reason that much of Eastern music originally used in religious shrines and temples is to our Western ears so hypnotic in its effects, while being monotonous and repetitious. It is not meant to engage our attention. Quite the opposite. It is meant to quiet our passions and permit us to turn our attention elsewhere.

Some may find certain kinds of music helpful to their meditative work. If they do, they should by all means use it. In general, it is likely that the more a person knows about music and the more he has listened to it for growth and enjoyment, the less he will be able to use it as a stimulus to his meditation. It is like any other intellectual and emotional activity. If it engages your attention itself, your attention cannot be turned inward. The music is one of the distractions. There are enough intrusive sounds as it is. Meditation is an activity that goes best in outward silence, insofar as that rare condition can be achieved.

TASTE, SMELL, TOUCH

These three senses seem more personal and physical. They have played a part in religious experience, and they still do. The Eucharist in Christianity and its counterpart in other religions like the mysteries of Orpheus and Dionysius, where the flesh and blood of the god are eaten and drunk symbolically, are to a degree taste and smell experiences. They have been spiritualized, in that the experience is interpreted as the incorporation of the god stuff into the body and spirit of the believer and, hence, the believer's attainment of god-nature. Millions of Christian believers in the modern world still find deep spiritual meaning in the Eucharist; but I think that even the most devout would not claim that this essentially ritualistic and sacramental experience is the same thing as meditation. So far as taste is concerned, if there is not a bad one in your mouth, go ahead with your meditation; but do not be distracted by thinking that putting something that tastes good in your mouth will make it any easier.

Much the same thing may be said of the sense of smell. The use of incense is common in many religious settings, both East and West. It is pleasant and soothing to smell a good odor. I can imagine that, if one becomes accustomed to a certain smell of incense in connection with meditation, one could find that smell a help in the process. But if this has not been our custom, the ordinary non-offensive smells of daily life are probably the best atmosphere in which to meditate. If we get involved in trying to improve our meditation by improving the smell of things, we are too likely to get lost in a side issue, an ornamental rather than a central phase of the whole process. Never mind the incense burner unless you feel you must have it. Then do not suppose that any kind of incense can improve your meditation. The most it can do is contribute to the atmosphere. At the risk of being impertinent, one can make bold to wonder whether the smell of incense so thick and overpowering in some churches and temples was encouraged there to overcome the stink of the poverty and the filthy streets outside.

Touch is a different kind of sense. When something touches us, we feel it in the place where it touches, but also in other parts of our bodies, as well as in the brain. All parts of our bodies have the sense of touch. Hence, it is more general and more pervasive than the other senses. The feel of a comfortable position or an uncomfortable one can have a decisive effect on our ability to meditate. The pain of a tensed muscle can destroy our whole frame of mind in a moment. A familiar touch of a known surface on arm or leg can be reassuring. An unfamiliar touch, even if it is not painful, can be very disturbing. The fly that lights on the end of the nose or the back of the hand is a real destroyer of concentration. Accomplished meditators have said that it is possible to rise above or move inward away from these small disturbances. One can reach a point of fixed attention where one does not notice them at all, so it is said. I do not deny it. I can only report that I have not experienced it. A sudden or unexpected touch for me annoys and distracts. When it happens, I must notice it, brush it off, or at least accept it. It is true that one can contain a specific itch, and it will go away in time. It is also true that an incipient cough or sneeze can be held in check and controlled quite often. A lot of our involuntary physical responses can be brought under more control than we usually exert. Each little success in these efforts is gratifying, because it underlines one of the basic assumptions of meditation, namely, that the individual is in control of his own being more than he realizes and can direct both his body and his mind far more than he has imagined to the purposes he wishes to fulfill.

On the more positive side, some people have found that the feel of something familiar and known in the hands during meditation is a helpful one. A friend once gave me a beautifully polished and finely shaped "comfort stone" that is just about the size of the palm of my hand. I have found that the feel of this stone in my hand did indeed bring comfort and reassurance to me. Perhaps the devout Catholic feels somewhat the same thing as he tells the beads of his rosary or holds the crucifix in his hand. Certainly such tokens are common in many different cultural settings. In most cases they can do no harm to the process of meditation, unless, of course, the token becomes more important than the process itself. But that can happen all too easily. People are always confusing rituals and symbols with the realities for which they stand and giving to the outward signs the reverence and attention that should be directed to the inner reality alone.

To sum up, any one of the five senses or various ones of them in combination can contribute much to our growth in meditation, but there comes a point where they must all be left behind. Meditation is essentially an inner work of the mind and spirit. The senses can provide vivid imagery and enrich experience, but at length they must become quiet as we try to explore the depths of the world within. This brings us to the wonderful and terrible world of thoughts, feelings, and the major vehicles for their expression—words.

WORDS

The five senses are the doors of perception through which all impressions from the outside world enter our consciousness. As they enter, the mind, so smoothly, swiftly, and automatically that we are often not aware of it at all, receives each impression, identifies it or questions it, classifies it in some framework of meaning, and relates it to other relevant impressions already there or coming in. The work of the brain in this day-to-day process is so complex and accurate, so suited to the survival and growth needs of the individual, that the most marvelous computers we can devise are primitive as compared to it. We have a long way to go before we even begin to comprehend the possibilities within the human brain and consciousness, what J. B. Rhine has called "the reach of the mind." Meditation is a journey of discovery into this unknown territory from which we have as yet only very limited intimations of what future generations will some day regard as common knowledge. One of these intimations is, as we have noted, the existence of an area, a whole world of knowledge and experience, different from the familiar area where knowledge comes through the senses to be classified, understood, and communicated in verbal symbols by the rational, discriminating mind. This different kind of consciousness does not negate the normal rational consciousness. Rather, it supplements and fulfills it. But to get at this intuitive knowledge, we have to make a deliberate effort to put aside for the time being the old familiar knowledge derived from the senses and reason. This is difficult, because we are so habituated to rational thought that we can move outside of it only by a sustained and deliberate effort. And, paradoxically, to move outside of rational thought we have to start with the symbols and communicators of rational thought—words.

The practical meditator finds that, since he cannot seek the intuitive insights that may be possible with a completely clean and empty mind, he must do the next best thing, i.e., use a concept or verbal symbol of the mind to bring the mind under control, strip down its normal activity, fix its attention first on one thing and at length on no thing, on quietness and openness to this different kind of knowledge and experience of which we have been speaking.

The great systems of meditation approach this problem from various angles. The reader who is interested, for example, can find six classical schools of Catholic meditative training. They are described in detail in *The Art of Mental Prayer* by Bede Frost. These systems are derived from the practices of the great contemplative orders of the church such as the Ignatian, the Salesian, the Carmelite, the Franciscan, and others. I will not go into them here, since it seems to me that while they have useful aspects, they are organically so related to Catholic faith and practice and expressed in such precise Catholic language that those unaccustomed to the style will be turned off before they are able to appreciate some of the sound and universal truths embodied in these systems. The same is true of other lengthy and detailed systems of meditation that I am aware of. The inquiring mind is distracted by statements of belief or descriptions of experience that is presumed to take place. Hence, contentious questions arise. "What does that mean?" "What if I do not believe that?" and the like. On the whole, it is better in using verbal themes for meditation to take something short, concise, and non-controversial. In general, the words used should set a tone, create a mood, but not demand analysis and criticism. Some poetry is good, since poetry tends to present an experience or an observation without argument, as something that is there for all to see. Brief sentences or phrases from the Bible and other religious works can be helpful. Also certain prayers and formal meditations are helpful if they are short and not provocative of contention.

I have included in a later chapter a number of one-sentence and one-paragraph or verse introductions to meditation. In selecting such material so much depends on individual taste that I have purposely made the variety quite wide, with the understanding that while some may be quite unacceptable to certain readers, others may stir something meditative in their consciousness.

As an aid to meditation it is helpful to have a sound and practical book nearby. I have included a list of possible books in a later chapter. This kind of reading should be done slowly and reflectively at the start and at the end of a meditative period. The best books of this kind are not those that tend to plunge into and wrestle with all the profound problems that are involved, but rather those that quietly relate real experience as simply and tersely as possible. Examples of classics in this field of literature are *The Bhagavad-Gita* from the third or second century B.C., a Hindu manual with universal significance, and *The Cloud of Unknowing*, a manual of meditation with a Christian background in fourteenth-century England. Each of these books has a crisp, direct style, with many practical suggestions as to how the beginning meditator should pursue his goal. They will bear repeated reading and offer insights the second time over that were not perceived at first. I recommend them highly.

It is interesting that each of the books just mentioned, as well as many other good manuals of meditation, come down to the suggestion that while words are helpful and even essential as a means of entrance into a period of meditation, they should be used as sparingly as possible. The Gita says that the single marvelous word or syllable "Om" is all that is really needed to draw and hold the attention away from the world of the senses and on the quiet unknown world within. *The Cloud of Unknowing* says that one-word meditations are the best. Use "God" or "love" or "sin" or some single-syllable word that sums up your condition or your desire or the goal you are seeking. Some Zen teachers suggest the single syllable "mu," which means nothing at all and is simply a word or inner sound that directs the attention of the meditator away from the distractions that so easily capture his thoughts, and helps to focus his consciousness on the self and its relatedness to the ground of being.

SILENCE AND OPENNESS

Beyond all words lies simple silence, perhaps the hardest state for a person with an active mind and a vigorous consciousness of the world to achieve. Little can be said about this silence and openness, because the moment one begins to talk or write about it one destroys the mood and obscures the reality. It is best to leave things thus: Sometimes, when one has been steadily meditating on one word or image or syllable, the constant repetition will issue into and merge with a great quietness and feeling of receptiveness. This may not last long, although if you check the clock you will be surprised at how long it did last. Time will seem, in Huxley's phrase, "to have a stop." At any rate, moments of quietness and receptiveness are what meditation is seeking. If and when they come, be thankful. When they cease, simply go on with what you were doing—breath-counting, repeating a particular word or phrase, contemplating an inward image or picture, silently waiting, or whatever. Such moments will return, if not that day, then some other day. Do not be impatient. If you are seriously meditating, you are engaged in a long and difficult journey in which great persistence, humility, and patience are necessary. There are no quick and easy victories, no dramatic revelations. If you find some, mistrust yourself.

Now we can venture to offer a simple suggestion of a meditation session that may be helpful to the beginning meditator.

Get settled in your place with enough free time ahead of you.

Read slowly and reflectively in your chosen book. As soon as you come to a sentence, a phrase, or a word that catches your attention, stop and repeat it to yourself a few times. Do not argue or wrestle with it. Just say it, think it, and savor it.

Put down your book, close your eyes, and begin your breath-counting, incorporating the word or phrase naturally into the rhythms of breathing. Refuse to get involved in analysis of the word or phrase. Just let it be and stay with it.

If you grow tired of repeating it, or bored, stop repeating it. Count and be silent.

Focus your attention on the word or the counting or the process of breathing itself. Close out everything else as much as you can. If it seems to be very silent, just follow the silence. Keep your attention open. Resist drowsiness as you would resist distraction. Keep your consciousness quiet, open, alert. If you begin to wonder what foolishness this is and why you are wasting your time at it, go back to your counting. It is your lifeline, your guide, your means of keeping in touch with time without letting time be your master.

You will soon learn to measure duration by breath-counting. There are many ways of doing it. For instance, I count in sets of ten as some Zen masters prescribe. I find that I breathe in and out six times a minute once I have composed myself and settled down. Thus thirty breaths come to five minutes and 180 breaths come to half an hour. This knowledge is not vitally important, and it is probably different for different people. What it does for me is tell me where I am in the time span that I have allotted for meditation. It also helps me to introduce new elements of meditation if I want to—a new word or phrase or a period of emptiness.

I have found that in harking back to the old tradition of intercessory prayer I bring into my meditation quite naturally people whom I love and who are part of my concern and in need of my love. I do not think my bringing these into my meditation performs any miracles or wins the attention of God to their needs, but I do think that it heightens my own sense of responsibility to them and my desire to make my concern wise and helpful.

I have also found that it helps to close the meditative period with some formal gesture of gratefulness or appreciation. You can call it thanks to God, if you like. I prefer to think of it as simply politeness to the ground of being.

When you are through, do not rush into activity. Wait a few minutes. Read a little more. Make a note of anything that remains with you from your meditation, even if you cannot recall at the moment how it got into your consciousness or what exactly it means. You may find that a day's or night's reflection will illuminate such details in surprising ways.

One more thing: If the session has been difficult and sterile, if you feel discouraged because you could not keep your mind on your meditative work, accept that discouragement; but remember that you have embarked on a long journey and that a lot of it is bound to be hard and tedious. It would be surprising if you did not wonder at times whether it was worth the effort. Remember that the people who have shown the way and taught it through the centuries in many different times and places have all confronted the question and have replied that it is worth the time and trouble.

It is impossible to be more specific than this about actual ways of meditation. It is one of the major fascinations about this kind of exploration that each person really has to find the way for himself. He can draw on what others have said and done up to a certain point. He can and should study some of the many ways and systems that have been used through the ages. But in the end his way of meditation will have to be his own or it will be no good to him at all. We can help each other with suggestions and advice, but each one must eventually make his own decisions and carve out his own way into the strange country ahead.

In two later chapters the reader will find a selection of sentences, words, and paragraphs that may help him in his meditative efforts and some notes on the literature in this field.

5

Some Further Considerations

GOALS

The practical meditator will find himself from time to time asking, "Why am I doing this? Why do I go on spending this half hour or so each day sitting around doing nothing? What good is coming of it? What good do I expect from it?" The answer is that goals of meditation are both immediate and long-range. Meditation is not an end in itself. The goals may be expressed in general terms such as a more orderly life, an examined life, greater collectedness, more useful and thoughtful action. Or the goals may be seen in more temporary terms, such as getting through the day better, reducing tension and anxiety, improving the ability to cope with stress. Probably the individual's goals at any given time will include both general and more specific ones. Their importance will vary in accordance with present circumstances. The busy person who works under constant stress and haste will feel the need simply to pause and collect himself so that he can deal more adequately with what confronts him. The person who has been seeking a more meaningful existence will see the process of meditation as a way of sorting things out and arranging his values in the order of their true importance. The person who has moved further along the road of meditation will see his goal as that of learning how to leave distinctions and judgments behind and focus on the intuitive side of his nature and its meeting with reality. From time to time it is well for each person to pause and assess his own goals. The evaluation may or may not mean a change in his patterns of meditation. If he finds that the pattern he has been following no longer seems to lead toward his goals, he should drop that pattern without regrets, grateful that it helped him for a season. If he finds that the pattern is beginning to bore or confuse him, he should drop it, too. But he should be sure that his boredom or confusion does not arise from his own lack of attention. Realistic goals are always in the process of change and development in the growing person. Therefore, we should not be disconcerted, but rather humbly satisfied, if we find that our goals in meditation are changing. That is the best evidence of growth.

PRAYER AND MEDITATION

We noted that meditation is not an end in itself. For some people who are trained and oriented toward a theistic view of the universe and of their personal relationship to it, meditation may prove to be a prelude to prayer. Prayer in our use of the word means sense of communication with a god who is in some sense personal, a ground of being from which or whom the individual draws insight and strength. Prayer may be naïve and anthropomorphic in the sense of the simple cries for help, protection, guidance, support so familiar in evangelical circles. Or prayer may be conceived as a sense of oneness with that power and love that lie at the source of all creation and all life. "We are all in him enclosed; and he is enclosed in us," said Mother Juliana of Norwich. "To get at the core of God at his greatest, one must first get into the core of himself at his least, for no one can know God who has not first known himself. Go to the depths of the soul, the secret place of the Most High, to the roots, to the heights; for all that God can do is focused there," said Meister Eckhart.[7] This is the mystical idea of God as the essence of all being, including that small portion of being that each person is. To discover one's identity with all being is the real meaning of prayer.

If you are put off by god-talk, however, you should not let that get in the way of your meditation. The reach of the mind is such that there is ample room for anybody to grow in his awareness of a physical, intellectual, emotional, and spiritual reality infinitely larger than his own identity, without being troubled by the god problem at all. Many will do best to dismiss the idea of prayer and simply concentrate on meditation as the effort to open up the mind and the personality to the as yet unrealized possibilities for growth already available to the patient seeker. If meditation leads naturally to prayer, well and good. If it does not, never mind. There is plenty of room to grow in.

INTERRUPTIONS

Anybody who seriously undertakes the discipline of meditation will find that there are various kinds of interruptions. There are the external interruptions like the telephone, the entrance of somebody else into the room, the casual question or comment, the barrage of noises that make up the background of even a rather quiet environment. These are only a few. There are also the visual interruptions—the sight of familiar things in a new angle or a different relationship to one another, the tricks that the eyes play when one opens them briefly after having them closed a few minutes, the further tricks of the eyes when they are directed purposefully toward some one object (as in some meditative techniques)—all of these can interrupt one's concentration. There are also other sensory interruptions: the internal activities of the body as they are heard or felt—the belch, the rumble in the intestinal region. In addition, there are the activities of the nervous system—the inexplicable itch of the nose or the back of the neck or almost anywhere, the muscular spasms or twitch that can be painful or merely annoying, the foot or some other member "going to sleep." All of these activities seem more obvious as we try to reduce the normal activity of the body, close the eyes, breathe evenly, center down our attention to some simple word, sound, or act, such as breathing. It is as if the whole of one's system rises in anger to protest the effort to control its many-sided unconscious and semi-conscious behavior. I know of no way to manage these discordant interruptions except to note and identify them and let them pass from one's attention. You may not be able completely to ignore such interruptions as the body presents, but you cannot let them become tyrants over you.

Even more numerous and difficult to control are the thoughts and feelings that come pouring in as you try to order the mind and empty it of distractions. One of the hardest things in the world is to clean out the mind and think about nothing at all or about one small and limited thing, word, process, or idea. Yet "one-pointing," as it is called, is the essence of meditation. It comes as a discovery to many who follow the path of meditation that it is possible to some degree to control the thoughts and feelings that present themselves to consciousness. We are not helpless prisoners of every random thought, desire, fear, or impulse that comes up out of the unconscious. Here, as with the sensations of the body, we must receive them, recognize them for what they are, and acknowledge their importance and their right to consideration. But each individual is free to make a decision as to where he will turn his attention, at least for the time being. This quiet determination not to be pushed around by one's own thoughts and feelings is the beginning of that ordered mind that meditation both seeks and flows from. We are getting somewhere when we are able to put our various intellectual and emotional concerns in some kind of reasonable order so that each receives its due and no one gets out of hand and becomes a tyrant. Obviously we never fully succeed in this effort. The volume of mental and emotional stimuli is usually much greater than our capacity to control them completely. But there is hardly anybody who cannot do much better than he normally does at this task, and nobody who will not gain calmness and confidence from doing so.

One of the discoveries that the practical meditator makes about interruptions is that, while they cannot be prevented and will continue to come, they can be managed and they need not destroy the pattern of meditation. If an urgent call comes on the telephone, you can take it, explaining, if appropriate, that you will think it over and call back. Or if the matter requires an immediate reply that is difficult if not impossible to make, you can say so. You can also let the telephone ring until it stops, which it will do after about eight rings. If the matter is important, the caller will try again. If it is not, you have escaped a robbery of your time which can be put to better use. It is astonishing how the telephone has established a tyranny over the lives of most people in our society. We seem to think that because somebody is able to make the bell ring we must drop what we are thinking about or doing and listen to that busybody, no matter how trivial his message or how important our previous activity.

Most interruptions can be quietly noted and put aside for the period of meditation. Then, if they need attention, they can be considered. Otherwise they can be forgotten. It is astonishing how many interruptions in our ordinary life can be forgotten without any harm at all to ourselves or to the one who interrupts. Furthermore, learning to disregard the trivial interruption will make you better able to identify the occasional important one when it does come along.

CATS AND OTHER LIVING THINGS

Early in the months of intensive daily meditation I discovered that our cat, Sarah, was interested in what was going on. She would come into the study quietly, and before I knew it she would land on my lap. Then, after a period of getting settled, she would stay there quietly until the period was over and I began to move around. Her demand for attention could be met by nothing more than an occasional stroke of one hand or the resting of the hand on her back or shoulders. The awareness of a living creature so sympathetically present with me in the process of meditation added a feeling of oneness with the animal kingdom that enhanced the whole meditative experience. It would be hard to convince me that animals, at least such an animal as Sarah, do not appreciate in some measure what human beings, at least their personal human beings, are thinking and feeling.

We have suffered so long from the illusion that human consciousness is something totally other than animal or plant consciousness that we are ill-equipped to relate to the natural world as a whole. It is interesting that meditation teaches what our growing concern with the preservation and protection of our natural environment insists on: namely, that we must learn to think of ourselves not as the masters of the natural world, but as creatures within the natural order whose claims to survival, much less distinction, are fragile. The practical meditator may find that the presence of a human being who is not talking, commanding, being active or playful or what he thinks of as cute, may be quite interesting and even alluring to his neighbors in the animal kingdom. Wild animals and birds will do astonishing things and move quite beyond their normal fear if somebody is simply sitting quietly in the midst of their world seeking nothing except to be.

READING

The practical meditator should keep by him a book or two that feeds his mind and stimulates him to pursue further knowledge. His choice of reading should depend on his own sense of his present taste and needs. It will do him little good to plough through a book that does not interest him at the moment. He should keep in mind that what feeds another person may not feed him. Also what feeds him at one time might not have done so a little earlier and may not do so a little later. Some books are lifelong companions, nourishing the reader more and more as he comes to know them better. Others are "sometime friends" like the chance acquaintance on the train or plane who communicates something of interest, delight, or wisdom and then passes on and is never seen again, but is remembered gratefully.

Sometimes in the process of meditation one is simply stuck. One faces a kind of blank wall, vast, insurmountable, forbidding, and discouraging. Then a choice must be made. Have you come far enough to be able to face the blank wall silently and perhaps for a long time, realizing that you may be on the threshold of a new kind of consciousness and awareness? Or will the effort simply discourage you? In the second case, take a book that you have found helpful and read a few lines until you come to something that engages your attention again. Then proceed from there with your meditation.

Teachers

Meditation is both an art and a science. There is nobody who begins and proceeds very far without feeling the need for the guidance of a competent teacher. Some people, of course, start out in a group following a particular course of meditative theory and discipline. But many more, I suspect, start out alone as the result of a felt personal need and something they have read or heard. They get along well enough at first, but sooner or later they feel the need of the support that a group can provide and the leadership and enlightenment that an experienced teacher can offer. In seeking to meet this need, one should observe the precautionary measures mentioned earlier and move ahead with some deliberation. Sometimes the best teacher may not be the one with the most highly organized group and the most clearly defined system of meditation. Indeed, such a person may tend to impose his own orthodoxy on one whose main strength is his desire for originality and freshness of philosophy and practical skill. The best teacher may be the one who is himself seeking and can share perplexities as well as knowledge and experience. The singular authority of some teachers may not be the best for some learners.

By way of general guidance, I once concluded during a time of great stress and need that I needed a doctor who was older, more experienced, and wiser than I. Eventually I found one after several false starts; yet I learned something even from the false starts. As the years pass, of course, it becomes increasingly hard to find a teacher who is older, but in the field of meditation it is possible to find quite a few who are wiser and more experienced. It is probably best in seeking a teacher of meditation not to get confused with the psychiatric concept of transference relationship between patient and therapist. Rather, the relationship should be cool and more objective than the therapeutic one often is. A certain amount of friendly distance enables the teacher to be more disinterested in his help to the student, and it helps the student to preserve his own sense of freedom and initiative.

The question of the teacher brings up the whole issue of the difference between meditation and therapy. Therapy inevitably begins with an individual who has a problem and a therapist who seeks to identify the problem and help the individual analyze, understand, and work it through. The therapist sees the symptoms and eventually their causes. In helping the individual to see them too and to get beyond merely suffering with them, he helps the individual to escape from their destructive results. Meditation, on the other hand, starts not with symptoms, problems, and causes, but with the way in which a person might learn to see more clearly, understand his own powers better, and function more effectively. Both kinds of help are important, and at various times we need one or the other, or even both. But it is well to separate the two functions. The physician or therapist identifies and treats the wounds. The teacher of meditation is more literally an educator. He tries to lead out the individual into a deeper awareness of himself and the capacities and insights that he has.

Personal compatibility is exceedingly important in the

choosing of a teacher. He or she must be somebody from whom you can accept correction and direction because of the deep respect you feel for your guide. Even more important than personal compatibility is respect between teacher and learner. The student must have genuine appreciation for the teacher as one who has gone further than he has and therefore has wisdom to share. The teacher must feel for his student a respect for the powers and potentialities that wait to be stirred into life. The good teacher is one who discovers, stirs up, and nourishes new life. His satisfaction comes from helping somebody to realize the best in himself. If your teacher cannot do this for you, he is the wrong person, no matter how gifted and distinguished he may be. By the same token, a person whose external attainments are quite ordinary or unrecognized may for a time be an excellent teacher. With teachers as with books we discover them, learn from them, and move on. Growth is a dynamic, ever-changing process.

STAYING WITH IT

Anybody who is serious about his meditation will experience periods of remarkable insight as the doors of perception are cleansed and new avenues of awareness open before him. He will also find a few rare moments when everything seems to be beautifully right as it never was right before. The disciplines of meditation will seem easy to him, and he will even be tempted to think that he is mastering the art of attention and concentration. But along with these brief moments of fulfillment, he will find many more periods of time when he must simply plod along as well as he can, uninspired and unrewarded, trusting that his steady persistence adds up to something in the end.

The only answer when one of these dry periods is encountered is to stay with it. The only hopeful news on which all agree is that if you do stay with it the period of aridity will end and growth will start again. The process is not unlike what one often finds in climbing in the mountains. There will be a steep pitch, and at the top of it one is excited to see how much altitude one has gained so quickly. But this will be followed by a long, slow march across an upward slope where it seems that nothing much is happening. But one goes on just the same, knowing that the slow upward progress is also part of the whole climb. I think that these variations in the degree of progress may be necessary not only to the preservation of humility, but perhaps even of sanity. If real changes are taking place in our ability to apprehend reality and our part in it, some time spent in getting used to the new perspectives may be necessary. One physician has pointed out that drugs may well provide people with some of the same experiences of enhanced sensitivity and awareness that meditative disciplines provide. The trouble is that drugs do it artificially and so fast that the individual does not have time to assimilate what is happening in him and to him. The meditative discipline that requires day-to-day attention, not only through the times of satisfying discovery, but also through the dry periods, gives a person time to accept, savor, and in a measure understand what is going on. He learns not only how to enjoy accomplishment, but how to be patient, how to wait, and how to persist when things are slow and stubborn. Both qualities are essential to a mature view of life. To stay with your meditative practice during the times when it is not particularly rewarding is as important as being there at the rare moments that make everything else worthwhile. In fact, one is essential to the other.

Satori, Kensho, Nirvana, Enlightenment, and All That

Sustained meditation carefully practiced over a long period of time is supposed to lead to some kind of fulfillment, an ecstatic experience of insight and enlightenment. I do not doubt that it does, although I have never had such an experience. From the point of view of the person who is in the early stages of meditative growth, it is probably best for him not to seek this goal nor to worry very much about how far off it is and how beautiful it must be. Like most difficult goals, it is well to know it is there, but not to spend much time thinking about it as one moves along through the early stages of the journey. The enlightenment that comes in the early part of one's efforts is likely to be quiet and slow, not a sudden burst of knowledge and insight, but a realization that important changes in consciousness and ability to concentrate are beginning to occur. The best analogy is found in the kind of bodily changes that take place as a result of regular physical exercise. Nothing dramatic happens, and you cannot point to any particular moment when a great advance was made. But the muscles do grow; endurance increases; the body becomes more trim and limber; and one tires less easily; one enjoys physical activity more. In somewhat the same way, as we begin to get our minds in order and our consciousness cleansed, we are surprised to find that we have more control over our thoughts and sensations than we supposed, that we can be patient, quiet, and expectant as the intuitional side of things begins to open up. We can be sure that the satori experience, if it comes, will be wonderful and ineffable. It will come when it is ready, when we are ready. But even when and if it does come, the main purpose of meditation remains that of deepening and enlarging our own consciousness and applying our knowledge and abilities to the understanding and enhancement of the quality of our own lives and the larger social life of which we are parts. As compared with this larger and more general purpose, moments of ecstasy, however satisfying, are incidental.

6

Meditation Starters and Sustainers

As we have said, the goal of meditation is to empty the mind of conscious, rational material, so that the doors of perception are cleansed and we are open to intuitive experience and understanding. But to make the mind completely empty and open is just about the hardest task anyone can undertake. One of the ways to approach this goal is to center the attention of mind, while quieting the senses, on one object, concept, word, sound, or picture of reality to the exclusion of everything else. This concentration in time will lead to the simple openness we seek. But we will have to practice patiently and be very persistent. It may seem contradictory to present a whole collection of words, sentences, and paragraphs that tend to arrest the attention of the mind rather than leave it empty and open, but we are word people for the most part. We must go through words and concepts in order to get beyond them. Everybody remembers those painful occasions in school when the teacher asked for the answer to some question and we stumbled to our feet and pleaded, "I know it, but I can't say it." I have not forgotten the teacher who stopped me in my tracks by replying to that plea, "Unless you can say it, you don't know it." Of course, that teacher was not concerned with intuition. Had I mentioned it, he would probably have dismissed it as emotional knowledge or self-deception. But he did express the prevailing attitude of the rational mind, and thus our need for words in which to arrange our ideas and impressions. Words are the natural symbols for conveying meaning and feeling. In the process of meditation we respect them, use them, and go beyond them to that other kind of consciousness, the intuitive kind, which is the place where words come from.

Most authorities agree that the amount of verbiage that goes into meditation, even if it is interesting and valuable, should be kept to a minimum. "Short prayer pierces heaven," says the author of *The Cloud of Unknowing*. He advises that the best verbal guides to meditation are short, single words like "love," "God," or some other short word that catches the attention and holds it steady. In this respect the fourteenth-century Christian teacher is close to the Eastern systems of meditation that offer mantras, or direct the student to use a single syllable like "Om" or "Mu" or some other sound as a guide to the fixing of attention and eventual cleansing of the doors of perception.

If the beginner can get along with this minimum of verbal stimulation and guidance, he should do so. Most people find it very hard, particularly if they are meditating alone and do not have the constant support and guidance of a competent teacher. For those who fall into this category we offer the sentences and paragraphs of this chapter. Brief phrases and sentences can be very helpful. You can grow familiar with them, memorize them, make them part of your consciousness. As they become your own, they will stay with you and light up various experiences and insights that come to you. Their intrinsic meaning will appear in greater depth. Some of them will become part of the intellectual and emotional equipment of your consciousness as it confronts the experience of meditation.

SENTENCES TO LIVE WITH

The list that follows is arranged intuitively rather than historically or in terms of fixed concepts and meanings. It is not meant to be exhaustive, only suggestive. Some of the selections are familiar; some may be new to the reader. Some are ancient; some are contemporary. Some are solemn in tone; some are secular, ironic, even frivolous. The standard of selection has been that each statement express some aspect of the perennial philosophy in such a way as to grasp the attention and focus the mind. The way to use this list is to pick out a few sentences that interest you and demand your attention. Then live with them in the meditative process for a few days. If you get tired of them or exhaust their interest and meaning for you, drop them. But before you do that, give them a chance to come to life in your mind, to rest there, and to receive your close attention. Some of these sentences may help you recall other sentences in your own memory that have impressed you at one time or another. They may even prompt you to create some brief meditative sentences of your own.

now the ears of my ears awake and
now the eyes of my eyes are opened
—e e cummings

No one who does not know God in this world will see him in the next.
—Al-Ghazali

Reverence for life. . . .
—Albert Schweitzer

I come in the little things, saith the Lord
—Evelyn Underhill

'Tis ye, 'tis your estranged faces
That miss the many-splendoured thing.
—Francis Thompson

When asked who he was, the Buddha said, "I am awake."

Only that day dawns to which we are awake.
—Thoreau

Know thyself.

—Socrates

The high road to God for your spirit . . . is the polishing of the mirror of the heart.

—Adam Sanai

In the midst of winter I discovered within myself an invincible summer.

—Camus

All deception begins in self-deception.

—*Theologia Germanica*

People ought not to consider so much what they are to do as what they are.

—Meister Eckhart

All the consciousnesses of my life are one consciousness.

—Teilhard de Chardin

If thy soul is a stranger to thee, then the whole world becomes unhomely.

—Kabir

In returning and rest, you shall be saved; in quietness and confidence shall be your strength.

—Isaiah

Keep your heart with all diligence, for out of it are the issues of life.

—Proverbs

Why should we not enjoy an original relation to the universe?

—Emerson

Blessed are the pure in heart, for they shall see God.

—Jesus

The kingdom of God is within you.

—Jesus

When you begin you will find that there is a darkness, a cloud of unknowing.

—*The Cloud of Unknowing*

The darkness and the light are both alike to thee.

—Psalm 139

The night comes, when I shall see.

—Anonymous

God is the denial of denials.

—Meister Eckhart

Nowhere physically is everywhere spiritually.

—*The Cloud of Unknowing*

God incarnates himself in man and evermore goes forth anew to take possession of his world.

—Emerson

The Word was made flesh and dwelt among us.

—John

God became man in order that man might become God.

—Clement of Alexandria

God can no more do without us than we can do without him.

—Meister Eckhart

Thou whom I do not know, but whose I am . . .

—Dag Hammarskjöld

Things are all the same in God. They are God himself.

—Meister Eckhart

The eye by means of which God sees me is the same eye by means of which I see God.

—Meister Eckhart

It is good if man can bring about that God sings within him.
—Rabbi Elimelekh of Lizhensk

On Me this universe is strung like clustered pearls upon a thread.
—*The Bhagavad-Gita*

I said to the almond tree:
Sister, speak to me of God.
And the almond tree blossomed.

—Kazantsakis

Beauty is truth, truth beauty.

—Keats

God is the binding element in the world.

—Whitehead

O my brave soul . . .
O daring joy, but safe. Are they not all the seas of God?
O farther, farther, farther sail.

—Whitman

Love rejoices in the truth . . .

—St. Paul

In his will is our peace.

—St. Augustine

Now abide faith, hope, love, these three;
and the greatest of these is love.

—St. Paul

I would be to the eternal goodness what his own hand is to a man.
—*Theologia Germanica*

Love, and do as you please.

—St. Augustine

He that finds his life shall lose it, and he that loses his life for my sake shall find it.

—Jesus

Between man and man is god

—Buber

All real living is meeting.

—Buber

They that wait upon the Lord shall renew their strength. . . . They shall run and not be weary, they shall walk and not faint.

—II Isaiah

Right understanding, right motive, right speech, right action, right livelihood, right discrimination, right concentration, right meditation.

—The Buddha

When once a man can see the diversity of contingent beings as abiding in one alone, and their radiation out of it, then to Brahman he attains.

—*The Bhagavad-Gita*

Do enough without vying
Be living, not dying.

—Laotzu

What does the Lord require of you but to do justly, to love mercy, and to walk humbly with your God?

—Micah

Whatever form (whatever god) a devotee with faith desires to honor, that very faith do I confirm in him unswerving and secure.
—*The Bhagavad-Gita*

Do not seek death. Death will find you. But seek the road that makes death a fulfillment.

—Dag Hammarskjöld

Send not to know for whom the bell tolls; it tolls for thee.

—John Donne

We are such stuff as dreams are made on, and our little life is rounded with a sleep.

—Shakespeare

And death shall have no dominion.

—Dylan Thomas

Let the night be too dark for me to see
Into the future. Let what will be, be.

—Robert Frost

What will you do, God, when I die,
When I, your pitcher, broken lie?

—Rilke

Yea, though I walk through the valley of the shadow of death, I will fear no evil.

—Psalm 23

He who would be victorious on the field of action must train in the fortress of meditation.

—Gregory the Great

In this life we find the time that is necessary for what we believe to be important.

—Douglas V. Steere

If a man does not keep pace with his companions, perhaps it is because he hears a different drummer. Let him step to the music which he hears, however measured or far away.

—Thoreau

Know this: though love is weak and hate is strong,
Yet hate is short and love is very long.
—Kenneth Boulding

I hope that the reader will be prompted by some of these sentences to add some of his own selection or creation. One interesting discovery after you have been meditating regularly for some time is the suggestion in many things you read that others are moving along the same path as you are. For example, a novelist like Saul Bellow presents his central character in *Humboldt's Gift* as an anxious, tormented contemporary man who is nevertheless trying to bring some order and peace into his life by meditating. He is not very good or regular at it, like most of us, but he is aware of the need, and he is trying. Bellow's own insistence on the importance of solitary reflection for the creative writer, and the concern he expressed in receiving the Nobel Prize for Literature that the notoriety involved might interfere with this essential meditative process suggest not only his own awareness of meditation. The successful novelist is read widely because he has touched some responsive chord in large numbers of ordinary people. As we move along in meditation, we become increasingly aware that we are not alone in our interest. Others are thinking similar thoughts.

PARAGRAPHS TO PONDER

The next section of this chapter contains a number of paragraphs that have been chosen with two aims in mind. They are descriptions of actual meditative experiences. They embody an awareness of the perennial philosophy through one of its key ideas. They can be used either as meditations in themselves or as reflections about meditation. The difference is an important one. If a passage is used as a meditation, let it stand by itself. Read it over often enough so that you are quite familiar with it; but do not try to analyze it beyond the question of whether the experience or state of mind it describes is something you have felt or might feel. If the passage is to be used as a reflection about meditation, tear it apart intellectually, find out all you can about its author and the context and the thought world in which he spoke. Compare it with others of the same period, as well as earlier or later periods. In short, subject the passage to rigorous rational analysis. Either approach can be helpful, but it is hard to do both together. Again, you will want to add paragraphs from your own reading to those that follow.

> We really only half believe in intuition. . . . But, in truth, it is available to all who consciously encourage and develop it. It is, however, in most of us a rare, uncertain, and timid process, that can so easily be edged out by the more pressing thoughts of our immediate concern. But once the ability to clear a passage for it has been developed, this awareness can become a familiar state. It will be received as experience, and not just as information about things; as a "knowing" that comes from a contact with the "known" that somehow short-circuits the five senses: and the confidence that accompanies its content is of a startlingly different degree to that we associate with the knowledge that is absorbed in the normal manner.
>
> —E. H. Shattock[8]

> Two major modes of consciousness exist in man, and function in a complementary manner. Since the dominant mode of our culture is the verbal and rational, recognition of their existence involves us in a cultivation of the second mode, the intuitive and holistic. The first mode is active, associated with our biological survival, the *day* in our metaphor. The second is receptive, and constitutes the dark, subtle area of consciousness, the *night*.
>
> —Robert E. Ornstein[9]

> This cannot be an easy life. We shall have a rugged time of it to keep our minds open and to keep them deep, to keep our sense of beauty and our ability to make it, and our occasional ability to see it in places remote and strange and unfamiliar; we shall have a rugged time of it, all of us, in keeping these gardens in our villages, in keeping open the manifold, intricate, casual paths, to keep

these flourishing in a great open, windy world; but this, as I see it, is the condition of man; and in this condition we can help, because we can love, one another.

—J. Robert Oppenheimer[10]

The most beautiful emotion we can experience is the mystical. It is the sower of all true art and science. He to whom this emotion is a stranger, who can no longer wonder and stand rapt in awe, is as good as dead. To know that what is impenetrable to us really exists, manifesting itself as the highest wisdom and the most radiant beauty, which our full faculties can comprehend only in their most primitive forms—this knowledge, this feeling, is at the center of true religiousness. In this sense, and in this sense only, I belong to the ranks of devoutly religious men.

—Albert Einstein[11]

I do not consider it as any part of my function to be a preacher. But it is necessary to say here that, even if mystical experience is subjective, it is nevertheless the way of salvation. That it brings blessedness, joy, and peace is the universal testimony of those who have it whether they are religious in any conventional sense or not. And though it brings "the peace which passeth all understanding," it is not, as is often charged against it, a device of escape from the hard realities and duties of life. . . . Here it will be sufficient to say that although mysticism can be, and sometimes has been, degraded to become a mere reveling in delirious experience for its own sake, this is not of its essence, and that the greatest mystics have in fact been great workers in the world and have recognized their duty to give to the world in service what they have received in contemplation. . . . It is possible that the direction of human evolution in future millions of years—if the human race survives—will be towards the spread of mystical experience to most men and not merely its possession by a few rare individuals as now. It is possible, in short, that the superman of the future is to be the mystic man.

—W. T. Stace[12]

The way of forms is based upon the predication: "Here is a truth: assimilate it; make it yours." The way of expressing starts out from the opposite prospect: "The truth lies within you, and you can find it only by forgetting the ready-made answers."

These are two attitudes that bear upon life in general, not merely upon the sphere of meditation. An extension of the assimilative and unitive approach is an attitude of respect for established forms and feelings of reverence for crystallized wisdom. The formalist is typically pious. The corresponding extension of the way of expression to life at large is that self-assurance and disrespect for established forms which is frequently part of the personality of a genius and has given rise to the stereotype of the artist as a rebellious man. By questioning established knowledge those who have followed the way of expression have been able to contact—to a greater or lesser extent—the sources of all answers without intermediaries, and thus have given new words, shapes to the eternal truth.

—Claudio Naranjo[13]

Siddhartha bent down, lifted a stone from the ground and held it in his hand.

"This," he said, handling it, "is a stone, and within a certain length of time it will perhaps be soil and from the soil it will become plant, animal or man. Previously I should have said: This stone is just a stone; it has no value, it belongs to the world of Maya, but perhaps because within the cycle of change it can also become man and spirit, it is also of importance. That is what I should have thought. But now I think: This stone is stone; it is also animal, God and Buddha. I do not respect and love it because it was one thing and will become something else, but because it has already long been everything and always is everything. I love it just because it is a stone, because today and now it appears to be a stone. I see value and meaning in each one of its fine markings and cavities, in the yellow, in the gray, in the hardness and the sound of it when I knock it, in the dryness or dampness of its surface. There are stones that feel like oil or soap, that look like leaves or sand, and each one is different and worships Om in its own way; each one is Brahman. At the same time it is very much stone, oily or soapy, and that is just what pleases me and seems wonderful and worthy of worship.

—Hermann Hesse[14]

There follow some paragraphs from some of the greatest teachers of meditation. I present them here in the hope that a taste of these great teachers will lead the reader to study their works more carefully.

The universe is deathless,
Is deathless because, having no finite self,
It stays infinite.
A sound man by not advancing himself
Stays the further ahead of himself,
By not confining himself to himself
Sustains himself outside himself;
By never being an end in himself
He endlessly becomes himself.

—Laotzu[15]

There is no need to run outside
For better seeing,
Nor to peer from a window. Rather abide
At the center of your being;
For the more you leave it, the less you learn.
Search your heart and see
If he is wise who takes each turn:
The way to do is to be.

—Laotzu[16]

Let the athlete of the spirit ever integrate himself standing in a place apart, alone, his thoughts and self restrained, devoid of earthly hope, possessing nothing. Let him set up for himself a steady seat in a clean place, neither too high nor yet too low, bestrewn with cloth or hide or grass. There let him sit and make his mind a single point, let him restrain the operations of his thought and senses and practise integration to purify the self. Remaining still, let him keep body, head, and neck in a straight line, unmoving; let him fix his eye on the tip of his nose, not looking round about him. There let him sit, his self all stilled, his fear all gone, firm in his vow of chastity, his mind controlled, his thoughts on Me, integrated, yet intent on Me. Thus let the athlete of the spirit be constant in integrating himself, his mind restrained; then will he approach that peace which has Nirvana as its end and which subsists in Me.

—*The Bhagavad-Gita*[17]

In water I am the flavour, in sun and moon the light, in all the Vedas Om, in space I am sound, in men their manliness am I. Pure fragrance in the earth am I, flame's onset in the fire: and life am I in all contingent beings, in ascetics their fierce austerity. Know that I am the primeval seed of all contingent beings: insight in men of insight, glory in the glorious am I. Power in the powerful am I—such power as knows neither desire nor passion: desire am I in contingent beings, but such desire as does not conflict with righteousness.

—*The Bhagavad-Gita*[18]

We are like a choir of singers standing round the conductor, who do not always sing in time, because their attention is diverted to some external object. When they look at the conductor, they sing well and are really with him. So we always move round the One. If we did not, we should dissolve and cease to exist. But we do not always look towards the One. When we do, we attain the end of our existence, and our rest; and we no longer sing out of tune, but form in truth a divine choir round the One.

—Plotinus[19]

One day Rabi'a was seen carrying fire in one hand and water in the other and she was running with speed. They asked her what was the meaning of her action and where she was going. She replied: "I am going to light a fire in Paradise and pour water on to Hell, so that both veils (i.e., hindrances to the true vision of God) may completely disappear from the pilgrims and their purpose may be sure, and the servants of God may see Him, without any object of hope or motive of fear. What if the hope of Paradise and the fear of Hell did not exist? Not one could worship his Lord or obey him."

—*Readings from the Mystics of Islam*[20]

Now let us mark: Where men are enlightened with the true light, they perceive that all which they might desire or choose, is nothing to that which all creatures, as creatures, ever desired or chose or knew. Therefore they renounce all desire and choice, and commit and commend themselves and all things to the Eternal Goodness. Nevertheless, there remaineth in them a desire to go forward and get nearer to the Eternal Goodness; that is, to come to a clearer knowledge, and warmer love, and more comfortable assurance, and perfect obedience and subjection; so that every enlightened man could say: "I would fain to be to the Eternal Goodness, what His own hand is to a man."

—*Theologia Germanica*[21]

When I speak of darkness, I am referring to a lack of knowing. It is a lack of knowing that includes everything you do not know or else that you have forgotten, whatever is altogether dark for you because you do not see it with your spiritual eye. And for this reason it is not called a cloud of the air, but rather a cloud of unknowing that is between you and your God.

—*The Cloud of Unknowing*[22]

If you wish to stand and not fall, therefore, never slack in your purpose, but beat constantly with a sharp dart of longing love upon this cloud of unknowing which is between you and your God. As you do this, do not think of anything under God, and do not let up no matter what happens. For this is the work that destroys the ground and root of sin.

—*The Cloud of Unknowing*[23]

Virtue is nothing else but a definite and measured desire plainly directed toward God for Himself, for God in Himself is the pure cause of all virtues. If a man is stirred to a virtue by any cause mixed together with God, even though God may be the chief cause, that virtue is imperfect.

—*The Cloud of Unknowing*[24]

People ought not to consider so much what they are to do as what they are; let them but *be* good and their ways and deeds will shine brightly. If you are just, your actions will be just too. Do not think that saintliness comes from occupation; it depends rather on what one is. The kind of work we do does not make us holy but we may make it holy. . . . Thus take care that your emphasis is laid on *being* good and not on the number or kind of things to be done. Emphasize rather the fundamentals on which your work depends.

—Meister Eckhart[25]

I have often said that a person who wishes to begin a good life should be like a man who draws a circle. Let him get the center in the right place and keep it so and the circumference will be good. In other words, let a man first learn to fix his heart on God and then his good deeds will have virtue; but if a man's heart is unsteady, even the great things he does will be of small advantage.

—Meister Eckhart[26]

If it is true that God became man, it is also true that man became God . . . and so . . . you haven't got to borrow from God, for he is your own and therefore, whatever you get, you get from yourself. Before God, work that does not come from your inmost self is dead. . . . If a man's work is to live, it must come from the depths of him—not from alien sources outside himself—but from within.

—Meister Eckhart[27]

Oh, who will give me a voice that I may cry aloud to the whole world that God, the all highest, is in the deepest abyss within us and is waiting for us to return to him. Oh, my God, how does it happen in this poor world, that Thou art so great and yet nobody finds Thee, that Thou callest so loudly and nobody hears Thee, that Thou art so near and nobody feels Thee, that Thou givest Thyself to everybody and nobody knows Thy name! Men flee from Thee and say they cannot find Thee; they turn their backs and say they cannot see Thee; they stop their ears and say they cannot hear Thee!

—Hans Denck[28]

A man saw Nasrudin searching for something on the ground.
"What have you lost, Mulla?" he asked.
"My key," said the Mulla.
So the man went down on his knees too, and they both looked for it.
After a time, the other man asked: "Where exactly did you drop it?"
"In my own house."
"Then why are you looking here?"
"There is more light here than inside my own house."

—I. Shah[29]

Here are some typical contemporary descriptions of meditative experience.

> First of all have patience. . . . You will disturb your development in a most violent manner if you expect answers from outside to questions which only the most secret feelings of your calmest hours can solve. I beg you to be patient to all the unsolved problems of your heart and to care for the questions themselves. Do not search for answers to be given you; if given, they would be of no use, for you could not live them. For the present live in the questions and little by little and almost unconsciously you will enter the answers and live them also.
>
> —Rainer Maria Rilke[30]

> The truth depends on a walk around a lake.
> A composing as the body tires, a stop
> To see hepatica, a stop to watch
> A definition growing certain and
>
> A wait within that certainty, a rest
> In the swags of pine-trees bordering the lake.
> Perhaps there are times of inherent excellence,
>
> As when the cock crows on the left and all
> Is well, incalculable balances,
> At which a kind of Swiss perfection comes
>
> And a familiar music of the machine
> Sets up its Schwärmerai, not balances
> That we achieve but balances that happen,
>
> As a man and woman meet and love forthwith.
> Perhaps there are moments of wakening,
> Extreme, fortuitous, personal, in which
>
> We more than awaken, sit on the edge of sleep,
> As on an elevation, and behold
> The academies like structures in a mist.
>
> —Wallace Stevens[31]

We shall not cease from exploration
And the end of all our exploring
Will be to arrive where we started
And know the place for the first time.
Through the unknown, remembered gate
When the last of earth left to discover
Is that which was the beginning;
At the source of the longest river
The voice of the hidden waterfall
And the children in the apple-tree
Not known, because not looked for
But heard, half-heard, in the stillness
Between two waves of the sea.
Quick now, here, now, always—
A condition of complete simplicity
(Costing not less than everything)
And all shall be well and
All manner of things shall be well
When the tongues of flame are in-folded
Into the crowned knot of fire
And the fire and the rose are one.

—T. S. Eliot[32]

Perhaps this is the most important thing—whether you work alone, in a group, with a teacher or in a school—to remain clear as to your purpose, to remain clear that the discipline is to help you find, accept and sing the best in you, a best that is unique, individual and yours alone. A best that you share with all those of the human race who, in one way or another, have made the search, but that is for each person something different and special. It is this goal and search that every great philosophy and religion believe are the highest and best things a human being can do and are the ultimate delight of God.

—Lawrence LeShan[33]

7

Reading for Meditation

There are many ways of reading. The first and simplest is reading for information. There is a certain amount of plain, factual knowledge that we need in order to live. This kind of reading goes on continuously and almost unconsciously. We note the time and place where we are to meet somebody and the purpose of the meeting. We note that we are expected to do certain things in certain agreed-upon ways. We read instructions, plans, and programs. In this kind of reading the meanings are right there on the surface. We receive the information, write it down in a convenient place, or file it in our memories. It makes no difference who the author is in this process of simple informational reading. It makes no difference what he thinks or feels about anything. We are not interested in that. We want to know the facts, and we want them stated as directly as possible. We do not want to know, for instance, what the writer of the timetable thinks about the fact that the plane, flight 69, leaves such and such an airport at 11:30 A.M. In fact, we would resent it if the author did include his opinions. They would only complicate the situation. A lot of the reading we all do belongs in this category of simple information. There is no problem in this process except to be sure the information is presented clearly and accurately and that the reader understands and remembers it, or at least knows where to find it when he needs it.

There is a second, much more subtle kind of reading that has to do with the efforts of an author to convey to his readers a story, an impression of reality, or a structure of ideas and feelings. Here the reader will have to deal with a certain amount of pertinent factual information. But he will also have to read carefully and absorb as much as he can of the author's manner of writing, the words and word pictures he uses to convey his impressions, and also who the author is, how he got his ideas, and what he wants to tell us, persuade us of, or help us to understand. In this kind of reading the one who reads must train himself to receive at many different levels and to make a concentrated effort to understand what the author is trying to say, what his values and shades of meaning are, and how his style may affect the content of his message. This is the kind of reading we do most of the time for varied purposes of education, appreciation, and entertainment or enjoyment. It includes much of literature, poetry, biography, history, and fiction. Somebody is telling us something that he wants us to understand, and we turn our attention to what the author is trying to say.

There is also a third kind of reading. Here, in addition to many elements of the first two kinds, there is a third activity. That is the active involvement of the reader in what is going on. For instance, when the poet Wordsworth tells me that:

> . . . I have felt
> A presence that disturbs me with the joy
> Of elevated thoughts; a sense sublime
> Of something far more deeply interfused, . . .[34]

he causes me to pause and reflect. Have I felt this presence that disturbs me? Where, when, and how have I felt it in my own experience? Do I feel it now, as I read his words? If I do, then the writer has done something for me which is better even than sharing his wisdom and insight. He has stirred me up to start seeking wisdom and insight on my own.

Reading of this kind cannot go fast. The best way is to read slowly, remembering that the purpose is not to hurry through the book, skimming off the best as you go, but to let the writer open up your own mind, and to follow those openings as they come. You may cover only a page or two a day at this rate; but keep in mind that this is a different kind of reading from the ordinary purposes of information, entertainment, or appreciation of the writer's knowledge and skill. Keep a pencil by you and underline sentences or paragraphs that particularly catch your attention and lead you out along your own ways of speculation or discovery. Read the same passage several times. Mark any phrases or sentences that seem especially valuable. Make them part of your daily meditation, not as puzzles to be solved, but as statements that you drop into the pool of meditation for what effects they may have. There may be none at all for a long time, until some day some one of the sentences you have included comes floating up to the surface with new meaning.

It is a good idea to keep some reading of this kind going all the time. It need not interfere with any other reading you may be doing for information, entertainment, or edification. It may well contribute, as meditation itself contributes, to your ability to follow other intellectual or aesthetic interests you may be involved in. The reader will find a number of books suitable for this kind of slow, repeated reading among the titles in the book list. The selections for meditation included in this chapter should be read in this way.

Selections to Read and Reread

Men seek retreats for themselves, houses in the country, sea-shores and mountains; and thou too art wont to desire such things very much. But this is altogether a mark of the most common sort of men, for it is in thy power whenever thou shalt choose to retire into thyself. For nowhere, either with more quiet or more freedom from trouble, does a man retire than into his own soul, particularly when he has within him such thoughts that by looking into them he is immediately in perfect tranquillity; and I affirm that tranquillity is nothing else than the good ordering of the mind. Constantly then give to thyself this retreat, and renew thyself; and let thy principles be brief and fundamental, which, as soon as thou shalt recur to them, will be sufficient to cleanse the soul completely, and to send thee back from all discontent with the things to which thou returnest. . . .

This then remains: Remember to retire into this little territory of thy own, and, above all, do not distract or strain thyself, but be free, and look at things as a man, as a human being, as a citizen, as a mortal. But among the things readiest to thy hand to which thou shalt turn, let there be these, which are two. One is that things do not touch the soul, for they are external and remain immovable; but our perturbations come only from the opinion which is within. The other is that all these things, which thou seest, change immediately and will no longer be; and constantly bear in mind how many of these changes thou hast already witnessed. The universe is transformation: life is opinion.

—Marcus Aurelius[35]

You will never enjoy the world aright till the sea itself floweth in your veins, till you are clothed with the heavens, and crowned with the stars; and perceive yourself to be the sole heir of the whole world, and more than so, because men are in it who are every one sole heirs as well as you. Till you can sing and rejoice and delight in God, as misers do in gold, and kings in sceptres, you never enjoy the world.

Till your spirit filleth the whole world, and the stars are your jewels; till you are as familiar with the ways of God in all Ages as with your walk and table; till you are intimately acquainted with that shady nothing out of which the world was made; till you love men so as to desire their happiness, with a thirst equal to the zeal of your own; till you delight in God for being good to all—you never enjoy the world. . . .

Yet further, you never enjoy the world aright till you so love the beauty of enjoying it, that you are covetous and earnest to persuade others to enjoy it.

—Thomas Traherne[36]

I left the woods for as good a reason as I went there. Perhaps it seemed to me that I had several more lives to live, and could not spare any more time for that one. It is remarkable how easily and insensibly we fall into a particular route, and make a beaten track for ourselves. I had not lived there a week before my feet wore a path from my door to the pondside; and though it is five or six years since I trod it, it is still quite distinct. It is true, I fear, that others may have fallen into it, and so helped to keep it open. The surface of the earth is soft and impressible by the feet of men; and so with the paths which the mind travels. How worn and dusty, then, must be the highways of the world, how deep the ruts of tradition and conformity! I did not wish to take a cabin passage, but rather to go before the mast and on the deck of the world, for there I could best see the moonlight amid the mountains. I do not wish to go below now.

I learned this, at least, by my experiment: that if one advances confidently in the direction of his dreams, and endeavors to live the life which he has imagined, he will meet with a success unexpected in common hours. He will put some things behind, will pass an invisible boundary; new, universal, and more liberal laws will begin to establish themselves around and within him; or the old laws be expanded and interpreted in his favor in a more liberal sense, and he will live with the license of a higher order of beings. In proportion as he simplifies his life, the laws of the universe will appear less complex, and solitude will not be solitude, nor poverty poverty, nor weakness weakness. If you have built castles in the air, your work need not be lost; that is where they should be. Now put the foundations under them.

—Thoreau[37]

O my quiet mind, do not fail to give me counsel more than seven watchmen sitting above in a high tower. There are bitter little moments when I think that if I had the ordering of this world, it would be a much better place than it is; and there are even times when I wildly dream of saving it from its ills by one terrific stroke. But may I not waste my strength in vain imaginings about the many things I cannot do, while neglecting the few things I can do. I would not shrink into the meanness which idly looks on while others do the work; nor would I become magnified into the posture of one who pretends he is holding up the sky. I would be willing to be counted as only one; but I want to be counted. When I see that there is a great thing needing to be done and that a small portion of it properly falls to me, may I not vote that a committee shall attend to it because thereby I relieve myself of all sense of active responsibility. In the spirit of cooperation, may I bear my own share of the load. At the same time, may I not take on too many things and do nothing well, and do some things so ill that others have to repair them. And let me not be quick to scold the world for being quarrelsome when my own behavior in personal relationships adds to the dissension. May I never be too weak to have enemies; may I never be so weak as to hate them; and may I often suspect that my own worst enemy is lurking within the walls which contain my querulous or my complacent self.

—Vivian T. Pomeroy[38]

Therefore the individual who wishes to have an answer to the problem of evil, as it is posed today, has need, first and foremost, of *self-knowledge*, that is, the utmost possible knowledge of his own wholeness. He must know relentlessly how much good he can do, and what crimes he is capable of, and must beware of regarding the one as real and the other as illusion. Both are elements within his own nature, and both are bound to come to light in him, should he wish—as he ought—to live without self-deception and self-delusion.

In general, however, most people are hopelessly ill-equipped for living on this level, although there are some persons today who have the capacity for profounder insight into themselves. Such self-knowledge is of prime importance, because through it we approach that fundamental stratum or core of human nature where the instincts dwell. Here are those pre-existent dynamic factors which ultimately govern the ethical decisions of our consciousness. This core is the unconscious and its contents, concerning which we cannot pass any final judgment. Our ideas about it are bound to be inadequate, for we are unable to comprehend its essence cognitively and set rational limits to it. We achieve knowledge of nature only through science, which enlarges consciousness; hence deepened self-knowledge also requires science, that is, psychology. No one builds a telescope or microscope with one turn of the wrist, out of good will alone, without a knowledge of optics.

—C. G. Jung[39]

I remember the saying of the old wise man, Lao Tse,
    "Muddy water, let stand, becomes clear."
Now I look within myself.
I see, on the screen of my mind's eye,
A stream of water
Moving, swirling, murky, full of things.
I cannot look into this water.
I cannot see my reflection in this water.

Now the movement stops.
The water is in one place.
It is heavy-colored, muddy,
But it is becoming quiet now.
The water is staying still and settling.
The heaviness,
The muddiness is settling to the bottom.
At the surface now it becomes clear,
Transparent.
I can see into the water more and more.
Now I can see through
To the very depth of it.
There it shines, and it reflects.

The heavens are reflected in the quiet water.
It is clear.
I can see the reflection of a tree in the quiet water.
The muddy water has become clear.

As I continue to look into the quietness,
A reflection of myself begins to appear.
Deep in the quietness of the water,
Clear,
A reflection of myself begins to form.
I sit in the stillness
And let the image shape itself.
It becomes many things.

Many images appear in the still water.
Many things come up for me to see
Out of the depth of the water.
And those images that open the greatest vision within me
Are not even those that are visible.
I do not see them, I just know them.
Something within me recognizes them
In the still water.

The muddy water has become quiet.
I sit gazing into it,
Seeing images, visible and invisible,
Letting them take form,
Letting them change and re-form themselves,
In the depth of the still waters,
In the depth of myself,
Moving, moving,
In the Silence, In the Silence.

—Ira Progoff[10]

To believe in God is not a decision that we can make. All we can do is to decide not to give our love to false gods. In the first place, we can decide not to believe that the future contains for us all an all-sufficient good. The future is made of the same stuff as the present. We are well aware that the good which we possess at present, in the form of wealth, power, consideration, friends, the love of those we love, the well-being of those we love, and so on, is not sufficient; yet we believe that on the day when we get a little more we shall be satisfied. We believe this because we lie to ourselves. If we really reflect for a moment we know it is false. Or again, if we are suffering illness, poverty, or misfortune, we think we shall be satisfied on the day when it ceases. But there too, we know it is false; so soon as one has got used to not suffering one wants something else. In the second place, we can decide not to confuse the necessary with the good. There are a number of things which we believe to be necessary for our life. We are often wrong, because we should survive if we lost them. But even if we are right, even if they are things whose loss might kill us or at least destroy our vital energy, that does not make them good; because no one is satisfied for long with purely and simply living. One always wants something more; one wants something to live for. But it is only necessary to be honest with oneself to realize that there is nothing in this world to live for. We have only to imagine all our desires satisfied; after a time we should become discontented. We should want something else and we should be miserable through not knowing what to want.

A thing that everyone can do is to keep his attention fixed upon this truth.

—Simone Weil[41]

Here are a few meditations that I have written and used at various times and in various ways. Some have been written for use in a group situation; some have been prepared for use in a weekly column I used to write. Some are much more subjective and express mainly the intense feelings I have had at various times about particular occasions and situations. I have found that it is good to write down this kind of thinking and feeling. For one thing, the act of writing demands a certain precision. For another, pieces of this kind serve as part of a personal journal that records not only external conditions and activities, but the way things felt when they were happening. Memory tends to grow dim over the years; but when you have written down the way you felt about something, a return to the written account will help you recapture the event itself and its impact on you.

If you decide to try some writing of this kind, don't worry about form. Put down what you feel and see in your own mind. If you want to polish your style and share your experience with others, you can do that later on.

When the Flesh Is Weak

Agony of body
Should not reduce mental acuity
But it often seems to,
Proving thus that sickly bodies
Can but do not usually house
Creative minds and souls.

I know there are exceptions
And can name some.
Still, I'll take a chance,
Turn my back on ancient lore,
And say that body, mind,
And what we may call soul
Are one and make a single being whole.

So my beloved and highly respected
Three-personed deity,
What do you make of that?
I'll tell you what I make,
Not that you can or will have time to listen,
But maybe you will.
Perhaps you inadvertently—
Or was it by design?—
Created in each separate segment of mankind,
Each individual man and woman, if you will,
The very triune person that you claimed to be yourself.

Hoping to hear from you soon, I remain
Your wondering creature and, I hope,
Still your faithful friend,

Starting the Day

As this day begins, let my body, just awake from sleep, be at rest; my mind relaxed and open like a quiet, unrippled pool; my feelings and desires ready and eager to respond to whatever opportunities the day may bring.

May I put off the darkness, frustration, and weariness of yesterday and, thankful for yesterday's joys and fulfillments, turn my entire attention to the day that lies before me.

May I receive this day as a gift from life and the deep mystery of things. Even though I dread some of its duties and demands, may I prepare myself to meet them with the thought that courage, intelligence, and love will help any situation and are never out of place.

If there are those from whom I should seek forgiveness and with whom I should strive for reconciliation, let me prepare to do so with humility and cheerfulness, recalling that it is not so bad to have been wrong as it is to have been wrong and blind. If there are those against whom I must stand firm because I am right so far as I can see, let me prepare to do that, but without anger and pride and with a spirit of firmness and love.

May I begin this day conscious of the blessings and strengths that surround me: the people who trust and support me; the people who put up with my foolishness because they believe, sometimes inexplicably, that I may at length become a little wiser; the natural world of air, water, and earth that nourishes and upholds me; the social and vocational world of institutions and responsibilities that requires me to give my best; the unexpected world of fresh insights and new encounters that I can never predict but can always enjoy if my eyes and ears are open and my heart is ready.

May I strive to live this day as well as it can be lived, giving to others the best in myself and, in the process, calling the best out of them.

When evening comes again, may I be ready for rest and quiet talk, for fruitful silence and the mutual enjoyment of wisdom, beauty, friendship, and love. When at last I am alone again, may I give thanks that another day has been given and lived as well as possible and then give myself to the little death of sleep undismayed, undishonored, and with a quiet mind.

Who Are You, God?

Lord, I do not fully know or understand who or what you are; and you must forgive me if, in calling you by an old name learned in childhood, I am making a mistake. But I have always been aware that there is something in the midst of life more "you" than "it," more personal than vast and impersonal. At any rate, I have found that when I acknowledge this presence, which is also a power and a purpose larger than anything that can be contained within my own small mind and heart, things go better. There is nothing miraculous about the process. It is just that I can do what I have to do and accept what I have to accept with a little more strength and dignity. Being in your presence is like taking a deep breath and filling my lungs with fresh, clean air. For the time being, at least, my mind is cleared of rubbish, and my heart is emptied of self-pity, trivial irritation, and small, self-serving thoughts. Our conversation—or whatever it is—makes me for a little while a better person.

Of course, it does not last very long. I soon slip back into my narrow ways; and that is why I keep returning to you, in order to cleanse my mind and enlarge my affections and my perspective. Sometimes, I must admit, I simply cannot get my mind composed enough and open enough to let your cleanness and strength blow through it; but this is, after all, my fault and not yours. You are always there waiting for me to be ready and open to your healing influence. It would be silly of me to contend that because my eyes are closed I cannot see you and, therefore, you are not there.

The truth is that you are there, even when I cannot or will not see you. You do not batter your way into my consciousness, but now and then you do give me little hints. Sometimes it is the moon on a cold, clear night, or the silence that seems to embrace me, or the weariness of my body, or the perplexity of my mind, or the quiet words of one who loves me. All these, in their various ways, try to tell me what I ought to know but so easily forget. The universe is larger than my mind can contain, more beautiful than I dare imagine, more pregnant with meaning than I have ever hoped, more alive with possibility than my dulled senses can feel. I am grateful to you for these reminders, so persistent, so close at hand. As a friend said long ago, "You know how busy I must be. If I forget you, please do not forget me." After all, we need each other. Who is going to do your work in the world if we humans do not? And how can we get it done without your help?

Connectedness

Let us try now, quietly and deeply, to realize that nobody is an island, that every one of us is a piece of the continent, a part of the mainland of humanity and of nature.

Let us remember that we are made of the same substances that make up all other living beings, all other human beings, the material world, and the sun, moon, and stars.

Let us reflect upon our connectedness with earth: We stand on its thin surface, eat of its richness, wonder at its variety and beauty, share in its fragile yet enduring power. We are made of dust and shall return to dust and shall be, from before the beginning to beyond the end, still part of earth. Let us have reverence for ourselves and, therefore, for earth.

Let us reflect upon our connectedness with air: In and out, waking and sleeping, we depend upon the life-giving vapors that sustain all forms of life. To poison air is to poison ourselves and destroy life itself. Let us have reverence for ourselves and for air.

Let us reflect upon our connectedness with water: No living thing exists without water, and our bodies are more than half liquid. Food we may for a time forgo, but without water we soon wither and die. Water is cleanness; water is flowing like life itself; water is life. Let us have reverence for ourselves and for water.

Let us reflect upon our connectedness with nonhuman life: Animals, birds, fish die that we may live; plants give their fruits for us; flowers and trees bring beauty and shade, color and form to our eyes. Being animals, too, let us have reverence for ourselves and for all life.

Let us reflect upon our connectedness with the universe and with space: the spinning world, the orbiting planets, the sun that gives us warmth and energy, and infinite spaces and universes beyond our power to imagine or describe. Remembering how small we are, let us have reverence for ourselves, because we are part of all this; and let us have reverence also for a cosmos greater than our minds can comprehend.

Let us reflect upon the connectedness with all things human: All men are members of a family, different in appearances, endowments, and with the accidents of birth and geography, but alike in the common human gifts of laughter, of cooperativeness, and of love. Let us have reverence for ourselves and for the humanity we share with all people.

What is this vast connectedness, as far-reaching as the most distant star, as intimate as breathing and the pulsing of the blood? What shall we name it: Nature, Spirit, Cosmos, Matter, Meaning? It matters little, but whoever pauses and learns to feel it knows that it is there and it is real. We shall call it God.

8

Living Is So Daily – What It All Comes To

"Living is so daily," says a friend of mine. Living happens all the time, today, tomorrow, and the day following. Whatever meditation practices we adopt and follow must find a natural place within the ordinary routines of daily life. It does, of course, involve the deliberate choice of quietness, separateness, and concentration on another side of our consciousness from that which is occupied with the activities and relationships of the day's ordinary business. But the influence of meditation should reach out into all the concerns that claim our attention: work, recreation, family, business, community contacts, politics, art, science, religion. Meditation will in time permeate our whole style of life, so that its insights and experience find expression in what we do and what we are. It should give to the whole process of daily living a sense of order and collectedness.

Meditation is, as we have said, a daily process of stepping aside from the immediate and pressing claims of life, so that we can "go home" to a larger life, make contact with a lost or under-developed part of ourselves, and cultivate a different kind of consciousness from the one we are ordinarily bound to. But the stepping aside is not an end in itself. The stepping aside is something we do in order that we may get a better perspective on our whole lives, including the world of action. There are practical and visible effects of regular meditation, but they do not come rapidly or dramatically. They are more like the effects of changes in diet or exercise. Avoid the crash program, and mistrust the promise of quick results, ecstatic pleasures, and self-transformation that come easily. But stay with a sensible, sustained, and integrated process of meditation over a period of months and years, and you will be surprised as you pause now and then to look at the self you used to be, at how much you have changed. We go on from here to note some of the changes the practical meditator may modestly hope for and expect in the ordinary details and functions of his life. People vary so greatly that we cannot predict what each person will find specifically. Improved functioning, better coordination, enlarged physical and mental capacity, and deepened insight and comprehension are general phrases to cover the kinds of change we have in mind.

SOME RESULTS

One of the first results of meditation many people find is the healing power of simple control and relaxation of the ordinary functions of body and mind. It is possible to control breathing and make it slow and regular. It is possible to sit quite still for prolonged periods of time without fidgeting or getting cramps. It is possible to reduce drastically the flow of sense stimuli so that the mind is more quiet and clear than we had thought possible. It is possible for brief periods to make the mind quite empty and open. It is possible to turn the mind's attention to one thing, idea, image, or direction and quietly hold it there for a little while. Each one of these meditative acts is a small accomplishment that carries with it a surprising sense of satisfaction. So great is the diffusion, distraction, and general lack of control of ordinary life that we are used to it and quite surprised to find that we can by our own wills bring some element of order and coherence into it. There is deep satisfaction in achieving even a little control of our own mind, body, and feelings. It is reassuring to discover that we are not entirely in the power of random impulses and experience, but capable in increasing measure of taking charge of ourselves. This discovery of unsuspected capacities is one of the first results of sustained meditation, and a very encouraging one.

A second result of meditation that comes relatively early is an ability to get outside one's self and eventually outside other situations that include the self along with others. It is possible after trying a while to think about the self, "this person sitting here," "this me," as "that person sitting there," somebody we can look at objectively and quite dispassionately, assessing hopes and fears, needs and capacities, with a minimum of subjective identification. Now "that self" there seems quite sensible and intelligent; now the same self seems dull and stupid. Who is doing the watching and judging here? It is a good question. The answer of unquestioning faith would be, "God, of course." But there are many who will know the experience and recognize it as something they have felt without being able to give that quick answer. They will tend rather to suspend any answer pending further investigation and reflection. That is the best way, just as it is best not to reply to a child's question with a quick, definite answer when you are really not sure. The quick, definite answer may turn off curiosity and further exploratory questioning. A gentle agnosticism and openness will leave open the possibility of finding more as time passes and experience deepens. The feeling of being able to look at oneself calmly and objectively as through the eyes of another is in any case an early and significant sign of progress in meditation. With it comes a capacity to stand aside from situations and see them with greater clarity and detachment. Much of daily life is reactive. We do not live deliberately, as Thoreau suggested. We react to what other people are saying or doing and to the external situations in which we find ourselves. This kind of living is not bad or futile. Much of it is probably essential to the conduct of day-to-day business and human relationships. Over many years we build up characteristic responses to people and situations which become valid expressions of our personalities. We tend to react critically or hopefully or generously or impatiently to certain events in the world around us. We do not plan these responses. They are habitual. If we did not build up these habit structures, we should have to think our way through countless daily decisions that we can now safely take for granted. Courtesy, good manners, the inquiring mind, the readiness to receive new people, new thoughts, and new experience—these are all qualities of mature behavior.

Even so, it is well at times to be able to stand aside from these habitual responses and consider them as it were from the outside. Much of the best in literature, poetry, art, and in the ever-growing body of clinical material about human personality, emotions, and behavior arises from the sustained effort to stand back, watch carefully situations in which we ourselves are to some degree involved, and ask what is really going on here. This objectivity and the deliberation that arises from it can often provide a new look at and fresh understanding of quite familiar situations in which we have been playing habitual roles and making habitual responses to expected demands for a long time. The meditator will find himself doing this double-take on ordinary life from time to time. He may even catch himself in the act of making some fresh and perhaps impertinent responses to stale formality or heavy solemnity. There is the story, possible, if apocryphal, of the skeptical minister whose doubts finally burst out one Sunday morning when, after repeating the Lord's Prayer for the 4,000th time, he heard himself saying, "So what?" instead of the routine "amen." Abrupt and spontaneous departures from established patterns may be disconcerting and embarrassing at times, but they may also suggest that deeper processes of reflection are going on. The meditator will find himself increasingly called to pause and reflect on relationships, acts, words, and routines that have become unconscious and perhaps quite meaningless in any sane view of life. It may be that some day meditators will challenge, arrest, and change the inane, knee-jerk thinking that leads practical and realistic people to accept and justify such foolishness as nuclear armaments, environmental waste and destruction, and war. The meditator can be a person who is going "stark, raving sane" in a mad, compulsive world.

We learn some things about time, too, as a result of regular meditation. At first it seems impossible to set aside thirty or forty minutes a day during which one will do nothing but sit and think, or perhaps just sit. It is not long, however, once a habitual period of meditation has been established, before we see that period of time as very important to our well-being. We feel deprived if circumstances do not permit it. Then we find that almost always circumstances can be arranged so that they will permit it even on days when we are very busy. Then the question arises as to what was going on in that time that was so terribly important. There is no more time now, of course; but something has happened to our perception of time and our use of it. Time flows more deliberately, and we use it with less sense of pressure. It would be presumptuous to say that we, the creatures of time, master it. Time will have the last word over all of us in the end. But perceiving its value and limits, we use it more wisely, neither squandering nor hoarding it, but moving along with it in friendly and expectant fashion. The wise and mature souls seem to have an abundance of time. They do not appear hurried. They live, quietly, at their own pace, and have time for what they find beautiful, interesting, or important.

To meditate requires steady and sometimes strenuous efforts at fixing the attention on one point. The fixing of attention on one thing means the deliberate withdrawing of attention from a host of other things. One encouraging discovery in meditation is that this fixing of attention is possible. One disconcerting discovery is that it can be confusing and even dangerous if it is carried over into the routines of daily life. For daily life requires paying attention to a great many different things at the same time. Think of the things that you must pay attention to in the process of walking down the street or driving a car. Think of the various impulses, ideas, images, currents of feeling involved in the simplest one-to-one personal contact or in the even more complex factors in a meeting of more than two people. Here the individual, if he is to function effectively, must be able to hold in his mind a whole pattern of different, often contrasting forces. He must be able to understand each one and give it proper value and weight in the total situation. Furthermore, these forces must meet and blend with the forces within his own personality, his own perceptions and intentions. All of these forces are in motion, and so they must be constantly observed, tested, as conversation goes on. This essential social task is very different from the meditative one, which is to put aside all such confusions for the time being and concentrate on one point. Hence, it often happens that the meditator will find himself in difficulties of memory and under-standing of what is going on. Given time and practice, he learns to move from solitude, silence, and intense concentration to effective functioning within a complex social pattern; but at first it may be quite difficult.

LIVING IN THIS WORLD

Once it is clear that both states of consciousness—the meditative and the social—are essential aspects of living, the problem of moving back and forth between the two can be solved. Many meditators find that their ability to concentrate on one thing in solitude helps them to find and stay with the main point in conversation, to cut through the masses of irrelevant material that usually surround the discussion of any subject, and to help everyone keep his attention on the most important aspects of the situation. For many years we may have been aware of people who have a special ability to listen to a prolonged and wandering discussion quietly, and then to step in at precisely the right moment with the insight that ties things together and makes it possible for the whole group to move forward in its understanding. I suspect that people who have this uncanny ability are meditators. Having learned how to pay attention to one thing in their solitariness, they have learned how to apply the same skill in social situations and help others pay attention to what matters most.

People who have been meditating regularly often speak of an increased enjoyment of the world of the senses. Nature, art, ideas, and human relationships all seem more interesting and more satisfying. Colors are more vivid. Music sounds better. The sense of smell returns. Taste and touch are rediscovered. Everything is experienced with a new sensitiveness, because the doors of perception have been cleansed. We do not gain any more time for living, but we live a lot more, because our senses are much more alive and open to impressions from the world around us. We enjoy the world more, and we sympathize with its needs and its sadness more deeply when we are fully awake to what is going on around us. Meditation makes people more awake.

There are also interesting effects of meditation on the outward patterns of ordinary life. One of the most important is work. The Buddha insisted that right livelihood was essential to right meditation, and presumably the reverse is true—right meditation is essential to right livelihood. What a person does for a living or for pure enjoyment or social usefulness should be an expression of the deepest part of that person's self. Too many people do not enjoy their work or find much satisfaction in it. They have been caught in their livelihood by rigid planning in their early years, by economic necessity, or by pure accident. Part of the examined life is the ability to look at yourself and your livelihood and judge whether they really suit one another. Continued meditation will almost certainly require the individual to examine his work pattern and decide whether, beyond providing him with the means of supporting himself and his family, it is useful and interesting to society and to himself. That kind of self-examination will surely raise the question of how much money and how many things are really essential to the good life.

My wife and I have developed a game that helps us to

understand and appreciate the simple level of material life at which we now live. We go through the ads of any one of a number of slick magazines and figure out how much money we can save by not buying things we do not want: jewels and furs at thousands of dollars an item; overpriced cars; vacations at resorts with people who have brought their own frustrations and need to escape to share with others equally fortunate; clothes and accessories that seem designed to demonstrate that the buyer is rich; insurance policies to protect us from everything including reality; investment programs to make us rich; and, of course, trivialities like a solid silver fly-swatter or a paper-weight certified to be made of an original brick from Independence Hall. We are not ascetics. We like to be warm, well-fed, comfortable, and even well-dressed and clean. But our society is engaged in a monstrous effort of over-kill in attempting to persuade its citizens of the importance of possessing innumerable items and services that do nothing to improve the quality of their lives and serve only to testify to the fact that they can afford conspicuous consumption.

The goal of right livelihood is neither too much nor too little, but enough—simplicity, the things really needful for sustaining life and providing reasonable comfort and enjoyment without the superfluity that makes possessions a burden and distracts the individual's attention from the improvement of his body and mind and the deepening of his consciousness. The goal is not impossible to achieve, but it may involve the meditator in some practical changes in his way of life. "Possess nothing," said William Morris, "which you do not know to be useful or believe to be beautiful." A good rule.

In addition to affecting the work we do for livelihood, meditation may also affect the quality and quantity of that equally essential activity, play or recreation. We should increase those kinds of recreation where the individual does something. To sing, to play an instrument, to paint or sketch, fashion metal or clay, to dance, to cook—recreations like these bring the person into the act of creation and make him part of it. He moves into life, rather than away from it as a passive, half-attending observer. In this area of action it becomes plain that the withdrawal from active involvement that serious meditation requires will eventually send the meditator back to active involvement in a creative way. He will be less satisfied with merely watching, more eager to take part himself in whatever art or science catches his imagination. Walking, running, swimming, sailing, rowing, climbing are all recreations in which the individual uses his personal strength and talents and finds rewards in the improvement of his body and the thrill of being a part in some way of the natural process. Gardening, cooking, weaving, handcrafts, ceramics, and many other similar activities recreate the human spirit by offering a contrast to humdrum intellectual activity and providing something useful or beautiful as a result. Thus, recreation becomes something more than mere escape and contributes to the well-being of the whole person.

Meditation and Health

Meditation, as we have noted, is an exercise of the mind and the will in controlling and directing our thoughts and feelings so that the senses are cleansed and quieted and the consciousness is opened to new kinds of experience. The body is so intimately and intricately related to the spirit that their activities and conditions are always merging and constantly interacting with one another. The experienced meditator knows all too well how a tiny physical sensation—an itch, a momentary pain, an involuntary movement, a slight cramp—can distract his attention and influence his whole mood. It should not be surprising, therefore, that regular practice in training, improving, and controlling the muscular and nervous systems of the body should contribute to successful meditation. This is the basic assumption of all the ancient and modern systems of yoga and other methods for strengthening and improving the functioning of the body. This is a vast subject, and the interested reader can study it in detail elsewhere. The important point to note is that sustained meditation will lead the individual inevitably to the effort to take good care of and improve the functioning of his own body. He will become concerned about sound diet, good sleeping habits, and a balanced program of physical exercise suited to his own needs and capacities.

Here again simplicity and moderation are the best practical rules. Asceticism is not a virtue in itself. Asceticism assumes that the physical aspect of our human nature is hostile to and destructive of the development of our spiritual and intellectual life. This is not so. Excess and superfluity are dangerous, but the body is as much a part of our total life as any other aspect of being. It should receive its due and be encouraged to function as effectively as it can. The practical meditator will make room in his daily schedule for a sane program of exercise. Such a program may take many forms according to the tastes and capacities of the individual. Some people do calisthenics. Some walk or jog. Some do various kinds of manual labor like chopping wood, gardening, lawn care, and numerous other activities that require muscular coordination and develop strength and skill. The main thing is to have this aspect of our growth in mind so that we would not omit it from the daily schedule any more than we would omit eating, sleeping, working, social life, or meditation. There is great satisfaction in the discovery that, even if we are well on in life and have over the years developed careless or destructive habits of bodily abuse or neglect, we can to some degree reverse this trend and recover or create saner and healthier physical conditions.

A word should be said here about overeating, overdrinking, and overindulgence of other kinds like smoking, pill-taking, and the use of addictive substances. A good general rule is that if a person is worrying about eating, drinking, drug-taking, or smoking too much he probably is doing just that. There is a large body of medical, psychiatric, and psychological knowledge and experience on all these addictive conditions. I mention them here in this discussion of meditation for one reason only: If any one of these conditions exists in a person's life style, it will interfere with his ability to meditate steadily and profoundly. By the same token, if the condition exists and the individual wants to change it and makes a start at doing so, he will find that a meditative program will help him deal with the condition more effectively. The meditative program will strengthen his awareness of the necessity and the possibility of his becoming the master of his desires and the director of his plans for personal growth and fulfillment. In short, meditation can be a powerful ally on the side of sanity and personal self-control.

Meditation has a crucial part to play in the achievement and maintenance of personal health and wholeness. Dr. Benson and others have amply demonstrated the specific effects of regular meditation on such measurable processes as respiration, heartbeat, blood pressure, and other physical signs. We are concerned here with more general and long-range effects. Meditation, as many meditators testify, enables the individual to live with a definite sense of well-being that comes from the feeling that he is in command of himself and his life insofar as that is possible. Hence, he feels not that he can control everything that happens or may happen, but that he can cope with what comes with reasonable courage and strength. "The mass of men," said Thoreau, "lead lives of quiet desperation." Meditation will not remove the causes or the occasions for quiet desperation; but it will help a person get through them better and worry about them less. Whatever in the way of disaster, suffering, and accident life brings upon us, meditation will help us to handle better. Whatever life brings in the way of happiness and fulfillment, meditation will enable us to enjoy more.

MEDITATION AND RELIGION

We come now very close to the essential meanings of religion, not in the sense of fixed theological beliefs and ecclesiastical rites, but in the existential sense of personal attitudes toward life and its varied experiences. One of the wonders of the world's varied religions and cultures is that the most durable ones, the ones that have survived, do in the end come to a common ground with one another. That common ground is love—a proper love of the self, which includes self-respect and self-development; a proper love of others, which includes kindness, understanding, harmlessness, and a respect for human personality; a proper love of the world of nature, which includes thoughtful care for plants, animals, and all the resources of the environment, since it is the source of every kind of life; and love for that strange and ever-present spiritual reality that seems to bind all our lives together into a coherent whole, the reality that we dimly apprehend in the process of meditation. The world's religions and cultures have created innumerable symbols and theologies to describe these sensations and intuitions. Too often these descriptions have been the causes of hostilities, persecutions, and so-called religious wars. These tragedies have happened because people have treated the labels and descriptions as real, forgetting that they are only symbols of the underlying experiences. The practical meditator will find that he has some symbols that he personally prefers, as well as some that he personally finds less attractive and helpful. He will, however, not let himself get involved in arguments about whether a particular symbol is "true" or not. No symbol in itself is true or false. The only question is whether it accurately represents for somebody the underlying experience of oneness—with nature, with other beings, and with the spiritual wholeness that includes us all. If any symbol does that for somebody, it is valid, it speaks his language. If we want to understand, we will not argue whether it is true or not, but rather try to translate it into our own symbolic language, which may, by the way, seem as preposterous to somebody else as his does to us. Beyond argument about religious beliefs lies the area where we can find unity of human understanding and participation in the larger spiritual life where all human beings are at home. This is the perennial philosophy of which we have spoken earlier.

What should such a philosophy or religion do for us? It ought to make us open and hospitable to new ideas and responses as they are revealed in all the different ways, some naïve and simple, some very complex, in which people try to express their deepest experiences. Such a philosophy may—I will not say must or even should—lead us to discriminating participation in some specific church or religious community. Meditation is not necessarily religious in the ecclesiastical or theological sense, but it certainly deals with many of the same areas of experience with which religion is concerned. Furthermore, most of the greatest teachers of meditation through the ages speak out of some religious background. They speak from a greater depth of understanding than is usually found in the institutions. That is because they are pioneers and have gone on beyond the average experience of religion. They represent a fulfillment rather than a contradiction of the norm. Like Jesus, the great teachers "come not to destroy, but to fulfill" the traditional and the average. Hence, the person who is meditating may find within organized religious circles support for his search and kindred souls who are engaged in the same search. Much will depend on the nature of the church or religious community. The advantage of participation in some kind of group is that often one can find people who are sharing much the same experience. Hence, it is possible both to learn and to teach in the process of attending meetings. The disadvantage is that meditation is such a highly personal process that many are reluctant to discuss its details with anybody except someone whom they believe to have greater wisdom and experience than they do. Such persons are not usually found in church groups, unless they are there as teachers or spiritual directors.

So far as attending services of worship is concerned, some will find the process supportive, while others find it distracting. It is probably futile to look for a church service that directly fits one's personal meditative program. Church services, designed as they are for a broad cross-section of people at different stages of intellectual capacity and spiritual growth, can hardly do this consistently for anybody. But if a church service can be approached as something that in a general way nourishes the mind and spirit while at the same time giving the meditator a sense of being part of a human community that respects his own search as well as the needs of others, then attendance at church can be meaningful. In a quiet way the meditator will help keep the whole group and the leader, if he is at all sensitive, at a higher level of communication. Perhaps the best reason for taking some part in corporate religious life is to keep the creative tension between self and society at work, so that we do not lose ourselves as social beings in the wonders and labors of personal growth. After all, what is personal growth for if not to make us more useful and interesting members of the human family? Contact with the group is renewing and refreshing. When the individual finds his meditation growing routine and stale, one of the ways to replenish himself is to move out into the world around him and involve himself in some real human situation where he can be helpful.

So Small—So Large

Meditation does something to our conceptions of the limits and possibilities of this life. Paradoxically it seems to intensify both the sense of immortality and our awareness of mortality. The incessant difficulties of meditation are not always profound and intellectual. They are sensual and bodily, too. The mind is persistently attacked by all sorts of sights, sounds, images, feelings, tastes, smells, memories. Cleaning it out and keeping it that way so that it is open to other and presumably profounder influences is an annoying, bothersome process that has to be repeated over and over again. A few minutes of deep silence and quiet are a hard-won victory. The body is no help either. It itches, gets cramps, feels inexplicable little pains, twitches involuntarily, wants to get up and move around, and in general refuses to be quiet. We are constantly trying to subdue it. Sometimes, when at last it becomes quiet, it is too quiet and we tend to get sleepy. These are all reminders of our mortality and of the fact that the human heart is, as Yeats says:

> . . . sick with desire
> And fastened to a dying animal
> it knows not what it is . . .[42]

At the same time, meditation suggests and introduces the awareness of something eternal. We are in the process of entering into a universal human search of dimensions of life and experience that do not pass away with the death of any individual, or indeed of any culture or religion. The dying animal aches and twitches. He is incorrigible, and it is all but impossible to get him under control and make him stay there. But making the effort helps us realize the fact that the animal shares in a life that does not die. It is not his personal life. Yet he shares in it personally, and that sharing illuminates the little piece of life that he can claim as his own.

It is November as these words are written. The leaves have fallen from the trees, and the fruits have been harvested. The branches are bare, and the meadows are brown. The nights come early, and the dawn is late. The signs of life and growth are making their seasonal withdrawal from the world in order that they may come again next year with renewed vigor and beauty. Our little life is very short, too. Longer than the life of a leaf or an apple, but shorter than the lives of many trees. But in the midst of that short life we can, by learning to use our minds and wills, by steady practice and concentration, participate in a much larger life that belongs to all the generations of humanity and contains all their deepest insights and experiences. These realities to which we can turn daily, as constantly as we wish and are able, can greatly enrich and deepen any human life, giving meaning and beauty to its brief years. Many a little life has added something to the total of the eternal years. Good meditation is a method of repeating the natural miracle of returning life within the human mind and spirit. It is a difficult road, but surely it is one well worth traveling. The views are splendid, the company good, and glimpses of the goal, alluring.

Notes

1. I have been unable to find the exact location of these lines in Santayana's works. I quoted them in an editorial in the *Journal of Religion and Health*, Vol. VII, No. 3. I shall be grateful to anyone who can furnish the exact reference from Santayana.

2. Huxley, L., *Life and Letters of Thomas Huxley*. Quoted in *Great Companions*, compiled by Robert French Leavens. Boston: The Beacon Press, 1933, pp. 322-323.

3. LeShan, L., *How to Meditate: A Guide to Self-Discovery*. Boston: Little, Brown and Co., 1957, p. 3.

4. *Oxford Book of English Mystical Verse*. Oxford, England: Oxford University Press, 1932, p. 116.

5. *Complete Poems of Robert Frost*, New York: Henry Holt & Co., 1949, p. 53.

6. In Huxley, A., *The Perennial Philosophy*. New York: Harper & Bros., 1945, p. 162.

7. Blakney, R. B., *Meister Eckhart: A Modern Translation*. New York: Harper & Bros., 1941, p. 246.

8. Shattock, E. H., *An Experiment in Mindfulness*. New York: E. P. Dutton & Co., Inc., 1960. Quoted from *Taking Down the Defenses*, by Arthur Foote, Essex Junction, Vt.: Essex Publishing Co., 1972, pp. 67-68.

9. Ornstein, R. E., *The Psychology of Consciousness*. San Francisco: W. H. Freeman and Co., 1972, p. 184.

10. Oppenheimer, J. R., *The Open Mind*. New York: Simon and Schuster, 1955, p. 146.

11. Frank, P., *Relativity—A Richer Truth*. Boston: The Beacon Press, 1950, p. 133.

12. Stace, W. T., *Mysticism and Philosophy*. Philadelphia: J. B. Lippincott Co., 1960, pp. 204-205.

13. Naranjo, C., and Ornstein, R. E., *On the Psychology of Meditation*. New York: The Viking Press, 1971, p. 129.

14. Hesse, H., *Siddhartha*, translated by Hilda Rosner. New York: New Directions, 1957, pp. 146-147.

15. Bynner, W., *The Way of Life According to Laotzu*. New York: The John Day Co., 1944, p. 29.

16. *Ibid.*, p. 55.

17. *The Bhagavad-Gita*, with commentary based on the original sources by R. C. Zaehner. Oxford, England: Oxford University Press, 1969, p. 66.

18. *Ibid.*, p. 69.

19. Plotinus, quoted in *Thoughts for Meditation*, selected and edited by N. Gangulee. Boston: The Beacon Press, 1952, p. 27.

20. Smith, M., *Readings From the Mystics of Islam*. London: Luzac and Co., Ltd., 1950, pp. 10-11.

21. *Theologia Germanica*, translated by Susanna Winkworth. London: Macmillan and Co., Ltd., 1937, pp. 31-32.

22. *The Cloud of Unknowing*, translated and with introductory commentary by Ira Progoff. New York: Dell Publishing Co., 1957, p. 69.

23. *Ibid.*, p. 90.

24. *Ibid.*, p. 91.

25. Blakney, R. B., *op. cit.*, p. 6.

26. *Ibid.*, p. 240.

27. *Ibid.*, p. 244.

28. Phillips, D. B., Editor, *The Choice Is Always Ours*. New York: Harper & Bros., 1948, p. 413.

29. Shah, I., *The Exploits of the Incomparable Mulla Nasrudin*. New York: E. P. Dutton, 1972, pp. 26-27.

30. Rilke, R. M., *Letters to a Young Poet*, quoted in *Taking Down the Defenses*, by Arthur Foote, *op. cit.*, p. 99.

31. Stevens, W., *Collected Poems*. New York: Alfred A. Knopf, Inc., 1957, p. 386.

32. Eliot, T. S., *The Complete Poems and Plays*. New York: Harcourt, Brace and Co., 1952, p. 145.

33. LeShan, L., *op. cit.*, p. 146.

34. *Oxford Book of English Mystical Verse, op. cit.*, p. 121.

35. *The Meditations of the Emperor Marcus Aurelius Antoninus*, translated by George Long. New York: A. L. Burt Co., pp. 161-163.

36. *Thoughts for Meditation: A Way to Recovery from Within*, selected and arranged by N. Gangulee. Boston: The Beacon Press, 1952, p. 69. Quotation from Thomas Traherne.

37. Thoreau, H. D., *Walden and Other Writings*. New York: The Modern Library, p. 288.

38. Pomeroy, V. T., *New Prayers in Old Places*. Starr King Press: 1955, p. 16.

39. Jung, C. G., *Memories, Dreams, Reflections*. New York: Random House, Inc., 1961, pp. 330-331.

40. Progoff, I., *The Well and the Cathedral*. New York: Dialogue House Library, 1971, pp. 15-17.

41. Weil, S., *On Science, Necessity, and the Love of God*. London: Oxford University Press, 1968, p. 148.

42. *The Collected Poems of W. B. Yeats*. New York: The Macmillan Co., 1956, p. 191.

References

Ballou, Robert O., Editor, *The Bible of the World* (New York: Viking, 1939).

Benson, Herbert. *The Relaxation Response* (New York: William Morrow, 1975).

The Bhagavad-Gita, with commentary by R. C. Zaehner (London: Oxford, 1969).

The Bible, Revised Standard Version (New York: Nelson, 1946).

Blakney, Raymond Bernard. *Meister Eckhart: A Modern Translation* (New York: Harper, 1941).

Bynner, Witter. *The Way of Life According to Laotzu* (New York: John Day, 1944).

Castaneda, Carlos. *Journey to Ixtlan* (New York: Simon & Schuster, 1972).

———. *A Separate Reality* (New York: Simon & Schuster, 1971).

———. *The Teachings of Don Juan* (New York: Simon & Schuster, 1968).

The Cloud of Unknowing, with introductory commentary and translation by Ira Progoff (New York: Dell Publishing Co., 1957).

de Ropp, Robert S. *The Master Game* (New York: Dell Publishing Co., 1968).

A First Zen Reader, compiled and translated by Trevor Leggett (Rutland, Vt.: Charles E. Tuttle Co., 1960).

Foote, Arthur. *Taking Down the Defenses* (Essex Junction, Vt.: Essex Publishing Co., 1972).

Frost, Bede. *The Art of Mental Prayer* (London: Allenson, 1954).

Furse, Margaret Lewis. *Mysticism: Window on a World View* (Nashville: Abingdon, 1977).

Hesse, Hermann. *Siddhartha*, translated by Hilda Rosner (New York: New Directions, 1957).

Howes, Elizabeth Boyden, and Moon, Sheila. *Man the Choicemaker* (Philadelphia: Westminster, 1973).

Huxley, Aldous. *The Perennial Philosophy* (New York: Harper, 1945).

James, William. *The Varieties of Religious Experience* (New York: Longmans, Green, and Co., 1902).

Jaynes, Julian. *The Origin of Consciousness in the Breakdown of the Bicameral Mind* (Boston: Houghton Mifflin Co., 1976).

Johnston, William. *Silent Music: The Science of Meditation* (New York: Harper, 1974).

Jones, Rufus. *The Luminous Trail* (New York: Macmillan, 1947).

———. *Spiritual Reformers of the 16th and 17th Centuries* (New York: Macmillan, 1914).

Jung, C. J. *Memories, Dreams, Reflections* (New York: Random House, 1961).

Kaplau, Philip, Editor and compiler, *The Three Pillars of Zen* (Boston: Beacon Press, 1967).

LeShan, Lawrence. *How to Meditate: A Guide to Self-Discovery* (Boston: Little, Brown, 1974).

The Meditations of the Emperor Marcus Aurelius Antoninus, translated by George Long (New York: A. L. Burt Co.).

Menzies, Lucy, Editor, *Collected Papers of Evelyn Underhill* (New York: Longmans, Green, 1946).

———, Editor, *The Golden Sequence* (New York: Dutton, 1933).

Merton, Thomas. *Mystics and Zen Masters* (New York: Dell Publishing Co., 1967).

———. *The Way of Chuang Tzu* (New York: New Directions, 1965).

Mysticism: Spiritual Quest or Psychic Disorder? Formulated by the Committee on Psychiatry and Religion (New York: Group for the Advancement of Psychiatry, 1976).

Naranjo, Claudio, and Ornstein, Robert E. *On the Psychology of Meditation* (New York: Viking, 1971).

Nickalls, John L., Editor, *Journal of George Fox* (London: Religious Society of Friends, 1975).

Ornstein, Robert E. *The Mind Field* (New York: Grossman, 1976).

———. *The Psychology of Consciousness* (San Francisco: W. H. Freeman, 1972).

Pascal, Blaise. *Pensées* and *The Provincial Letters* (New York: Modern Library, 1941).

Phillips, Dorothy Berkley, Editor, *The Choice Is Always Ours* (New York: Harper, 1960).

Pomeroy, Vivian T. *New Prayers in Old Places* (Boston: The Beacon Press, 1955).

Progoff, Ira. *The Well and the Cathedral* (New York: Dialogue House Library, 1971).

Ross, Nancy Wilson, Editor, *The World of Zen: An East-West Anthology* (New York: Vintage Books, 1960).

Shah, Idries. *The Dermis Probe* (New York: Dutton, 1971).

———. *The Exploits of the Incomparable Mulla Nasrudin* (New York: Dutton, 1972).

———. *The Pleasantries of the Incredible Mulla Nasrudin* (New York: Dutton, 1971).

———. *Thinkers of the East* (Baltimore: Penguin, 1973).

———. *The Way of the Sufi* (New York: Dutton, 1970).

———. *Wisdom of the Idiots* (New York: Dutton, 1971).

Shattock, E. H. *An Experiment in Mindfulness* (New York: Dutton, 1960).

Smith, Margaret. *Readings from the Mystics of Islam* (London: Luzac, 1950).

The Sound of One Hand: 280 Zen Koans with Answers, translated with a commentary by Yoel Hoffman (New York: Basic Books, 1975).

Stace, W. T. *Mysticism and Philosophy* (Philadelphia: Lippincott, 1960).

Steere, Douglas V. *Prayer and Worship* (New York: Association Press, 1938).

———. *Time to Spare* (New York: Harper, 1949).

———. *Work and Contemplation* (New York: Harper, 1957).

Stiernotte, Alfred P., Editor, *Mysticism and the Modern Mind* (New York: Liberal Arts Press, 1959).

Stryk, Lucien, Editor, *World of the Buddha* (Garden City: Doubleday, 1968).

Suzuki, D. T. *Mysticism: Christian and Buddhist* (New York: Harper, 1957).

———, with Fromm, E., and de Martino, R. *Zen Buddhism and Psychoanalysis* (New York: Harper, 1960).

Suzuki, Shunryu. *Zen Mind, Beginner's Mind* (New York: John Weatherhill, 1970).

Theologia Germanica, translated by Susanna Winkworth (London: Macmillan, 1937).

Thich Nhat Hanh. *The Miracle of Mindfulness: A Manual on Meditation* (Boston: Beacon Press, 1976).

Thoreau, Henry David. *Walden and Other Writings* (New York: Modern Library).

Thoughts for Meditation, selected and arranged by N. Gangulee (Boston: Beacon Press, 1952).

Vining, Elizabeth Gray. *The World in Tune* (New York: Harper, 1954).

Weil, Simone. *On Science, Necessity and the Love of God* (London: Oxford, 1968).

————. *The Simone Weil Reader* (New York: McKay, 1977).

Weitzner, Emil. *Humanist Meditations and Paraphrases* (New York: Random House, 1965).

Index